Conker Editions Ltd
22 Cosby Road
Littlethorpe
Leicester LE19 2HF
Email: books@conkereditions.co.uk
Website: www.conkereditions.co.uk
First published by Conker Editions Ltd 2025.
Text © 2025 Bill Hern, Derek Hammond & Gary Silke.
Bill Hern, Derek Hammond & Gary Silke have asserted their rights in accordance with the Copyright, Designs and Patents Act 1988 to be identified as the author of this work. All rights reserved. No part of this publication may be reproduced, stored in a retrieval system, or transmitted in any form or by any means, electronic, mechanical, photocopying, recording or otherwise, without the prior permission in writing of the publisher and the copyright owners, or as expressly permitted by law, or under terms agreed with the appropriate reprographics rights organisation. Enquiries concerning reproduction outside the terms stated here should be sent to the publishers at the UK address printed on this page.
The publisher makes no representation, express or implied, with regard to the accuracy of the information contained in this book and cannot accept any legal responsibility for any errors or omissions that may be made.
A CIP catalogue record for this book is available from the British Library.
13-digit ISBN: 978-1-0687009-2-7.
Design and typesetting by Gary Silke.
Printed in the UK by Mixam.

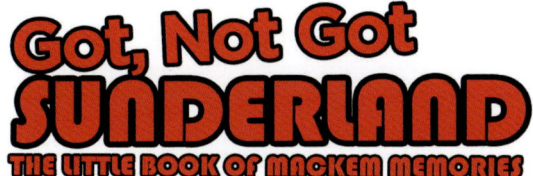

Got, Not Got SUNDERLAND
THE LITTLE BOOK OF MACKEM MEMORIES

**Bill Hern,
Derek Hammond & Gary Silke**

INTRODUCTION

I heard this plea from my two sons more than once in the early '90s as we trudged from a rapidly decaying Roker Park after another miserable performance: "Oh dad, why did we have to be born in Sunderland? Couldn't we have been born in Liverpool or Manchester?"

And yet, along with the misery, I felt a sense of real pride.

It never crossed their minds to switch allegiance to a so-called 'glamour' club. Sunderland fans are born, not made. As the saying goes; 'Sunderland 'til I Die.'

I started following Sunderland in the 1963/64 promotion-winning season but wasn't allowed to go to a 'big' game until Good Friday 1965. A win would ensure we avoided relegation but virtually consign our opponents, Wolves, to the Second Division. Mike Hellawell scored for us in the very first minute. Was this a sign of things to come? Well, in a way it was, because we lost 2-1.

We stayed up by beating Birmingham City the following day, one of three games in five days – don't talk to me about fixture congestion! Despite beating us again by three goals to nil on Easter Tuesday, Wolves couldn't beat the drop.

Trophies were few and far between, to say the least, in the last 30 years of the 20th century. Personally, I wouldn't swap the 1973 FA Cup final win for a dozen League Cups. What a special day that was. And what a special city and club Sunderland is.

I moved to Leeds in 1992 and for a couple of seasons we had season tickets for Elland Road and Roker Park. It gave my sons the chance to watch Premiership football but, apart from when Leeds played the Magpies, we could feel no real passion or sense of belonging. As Niall Quinn famously said; "I learned my trade at Arsenal, became a footballer at Manchester City, but Sunderland got under my skin."

Even at our lowest ebb we have always been recognised as a big club, steeped in a rich history with a huge and faithful following. I hope this book rekindles good and happy memories and reminds us all why we are Sunderland 'til We Die.

Bill

A&BC Football Cards

Back in the 1950s, A&BC Chewing Gum of Romford, Essex, made a rather special contribution to the history of childhood and football alike. They came up with the idea of packaging together two completely unrelated items, in a way that would henceforward be considered a perfectly natural and obvious fit: they bunged a thin slab of fossilised chewing gum into a pack of football cards.

The value of these cards, especially the rarer ones from the early and mid '60s but also the standard '70s issues, has risen exponentially in recent years, so that the eBay sale of certain individual cards from the super-sought-after Scottish sets or star-player rookie cards could easily pay off your mortgage. Provided they're in excellent condition, that is – sadly, values drop off steeply for ones with the edges chewed and worn, like ours.

The 'crinkle-cut' extra photographs given away free with each pack in 1969 are even more desirable, and the little Action Transfers given away as extras in every pack in 1971 can be worth well into double figures apiece. This for a small piece of paper

that was given away in a packet that cost thruppence.

Even more amazing and frustrating, in retrospect, is the fact that neither the cards nor the giveaways were the real prizes in the A&BC package. That honour goes to the wax-paper wrapper itself, automatically thrown in the newsagent's bin or to the playground Tarmac back in the day... hence their massive rarity and spiralling value to obsessive collectors.

Sadly, in 1974, A&BC lost a long legal battle and was taken over by Topps-Bazooka.

End of story.

But, for some reason, it isn't easy to put out of your mind ancient rituals of needing and swapping, much less stray memories of long-lost heroes. The names and faces always stay with you, and have the magical power to make you sigh. Ahhh... whatever happened to Gordon Harris? AKA 'Grandad' – because kids on the terraces thought he looked old for his 29 years...

Car Decorations

Sometimes you remember something that seems so outlandish, you think you must have imagined it; but I've checked and, yes, in the '70s, '80s and early '90s, many people decorated their car with a pair of giant die (as in the plural for dice). They would hang from the mirror and make a 'statement', though I'm not sure the one intended was to tell everyone that the driver was a pillock and the car would most certainly fail its MOT if they didn't remove said large, sometimes furry, dice.

Often the die would be accompanied by an adhesive

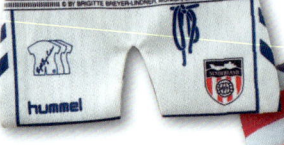

strip on the top of the windscreen showing the name of the driver (often Darren) and his passenger (Sharon was a popular one). Funny how the driver was always male.

But it's the back of the car that we're now

most interested in. Whereas the front exhibited your allegiance and love for your partner, the back of the car did the same for your football club. A miniature team strip would be affixed to the rear window by wetting a sucker and pressing it on to the glass. You could then drive safe in the knowledge that anyone close enough to your rear bumper knew how proud you were to support your club.

Another worry was away games. You certainly didn't want to leave your car in a dodgy Birmingham backstreet with a Sunderland strip hanging from your rear window. Off would come the miniature strip to be deposited in the glove compartment until the long journey home. The names on the front windscreen weren't a risk unless you came across someone with a pathological hatred of anyone with the name Darren or Sharon...

Ty-Phoo Tea

It's the cross that every 20th Century Boy has to bear. Having been brought up in the greatest era for football giveaways as well as for football, we can't help feeling just a little bit cheated these days when all of the stuff we buy doesn't come with something free bundled inside.

Cereal packets don't come with little presents inside any more. Four gallons of 4-star petrol don't bring with them a World Cup coin. Comics don't have goodies stuck to the cover, and trade cards aren't given away with everything from tea and ciggies (remember them?) to ice-cream.

WITH THE COMPLIMENTS OF Ty-Phoo TEA LTD., BIRMINGHAM 5

SUNDERLAND F.C.
Back row, L to R: McNab, Parke, Harvey, McLaughlan, Hurley, Ashurst, Irwin
Front row, L to R: Heliawell, Herd, Hood, Sharkey, Mulhall

In the '60s, those nice people at Ty-Phoo Tea were running a smashing offer whereby any thirsty fan could collect up packet tops and send off for a large

10" by 8" teamgroup card of their choice.

And sometimes you'd even get a little collector card of a player printed on the side of the box, which kids would inevitably hack out with scissors before their mam could get the tea (note, that's 'tea', not your common-as-muck not-yet-invented 'teabags') into the tea canister.

League Ladders

Wahey! Sunderland top of the League! Who could ever resist the youthful flight of fancy that involved plucking the Sunderland team tab from wherever we'd yo-yo'd at the end of the previous season, and placing it boldly where it rightfully belonged – all things considered – at the top of the League.

Of course, there was more to league ladder-related fantasy than self-centred, feelgood relish. There was also the bottom of the basement to consider. That's where a good old-fashioned English emotion known as *schadenfreude* took over – and where you found clustered the likes of Manchester United, Liverpool and any other team that had jammily managed to put one over on the Lads in recent seasons.

Gifted to us in the build-up to the season's big kick-off by *Shoot!* or *Roy of the Rovers,* the empty league ladders came first, closely followed over a number of weeks with the small cardboard team tabs designed to be slipped into their ever-changing slot in

scheme of things. In the days before Ceefax and computers, it was a novelty to be able to check league positions. But, after the third or fourth week, updating your league ladders became a bit too much like hard work.

And that's when Newcastle United discovered how it felt to hit bottom spot... in Scottish League Division Two.

SHOOT

1st DIVISION

1. SUNDERLAND
2. EVERTON
3. LIVERPOOL
4. MANCHESTER U.
5. MANCHESTER C.
6. ARSENAL
7. DERBY
8. LEEDS
9. IPSWICH
10. STOKE
11. WEST HAM
12. COVENTRY
13. SOUTHAMPTON
14. WEST BROM
15. TOTTENHAM
16. LEICESTER
17. QUEEN'S P.R.
18. WOLVES
19. ASTON VILLA
20. NORWICH
21. MIDDLESBRO'
22. NEWCASTLE

Pro Set

Some time after the Golden Age of football cards, a new collection made by Pro Set was suddenly launched during the 1990/91 season. They were a good-looking series covering Sunderland's chevron-happy Hummel period, and a second series was brought out the following season.

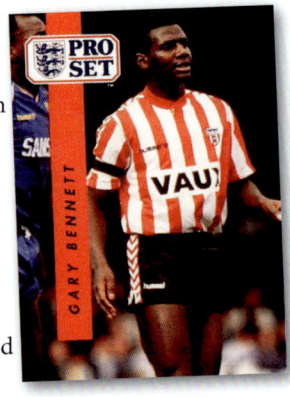

For a short time, the modern dominance of the sticker albums was, well, not exactly threatened, but certainly given a run for its money in terms of quality and feel when flicking through the swap pile.

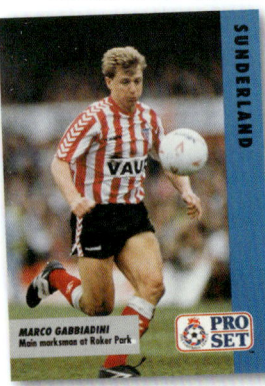

The landmark first set was branded with the FA badge and the second carried the Football League logo, though that belaboured institution was on the verge of losing all of its biggest clubs to the newly formed

Premier League. As a result, we're still awaiting the appearance of a third collection.

Only with the advent of the internet did we discover that Pro Set was a US company belonging to Lud Denny, a former pilot and oil operator who took a punt on producing sports cards and ending up doing $165 million of business in a year.

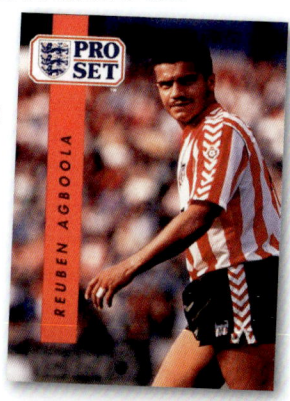

Somewhat cryptically, Mr Denny said of his 44,000-square-foot Dallas HQ: "We're getting to be a reasonably sized lemonade stand."

After producing cards for American football, hockey and golf he turned his attention to 'soccer'.

It appears Lud had learned a lesson from the generation before him as his marketing plan closely resembled the US Army's operation against Hitler: "Basically, England is a stepping stone into the rest of Europe..."

Super Striker

for anyone who only ever played Striker with the random teams provided in the standard, original game, it's quite sickening to discover – albeit 50 years too late – that a whole extra range of enviable, individual team sets were introduced by Palitoy in 1977, as part of the Super Striker range with the Astroturf pitch and built-in pitch barrier aimed at posh kids.

It's even more sickening to take on board the information that Sunderland were not one of the teams blessed with inclusion, as Palitoy were clearly

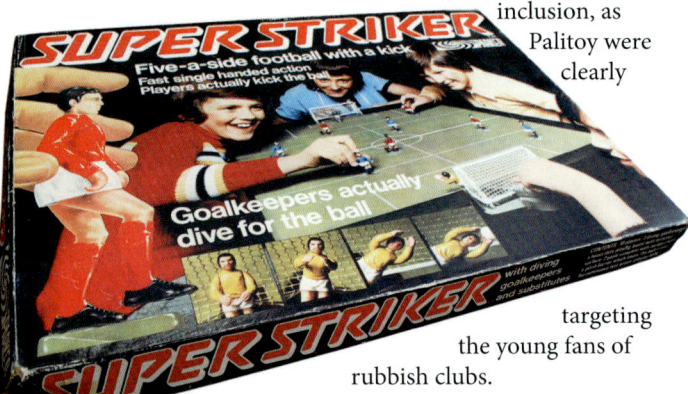

targeting the young fans of rubbish clubs.

It isn't quite so hurtful when you hear this late, late news direct from Striker aficionado James Hills, who will soon turn out to be the hero of this story.

"The All-star range had modern-looking kits such as Newcastle and Man United as well as ones that looked like Crystal Palace, Ipswich Town and/or Everton,

Middlesbrough, Leeds United away, Birmingham and Coventry City away...

"Then things moved on to another level when actual teams came out. Liverpool, Everton, Spurs, Man City, Arsenal, Forest, Villa and Leeds teams meant you could play out a whole league fixture list."

The good news is that James was also a dab hand at painting his own custom teams – including Sunderland, at long last! One of whom looked curiously like Graeme Souness...

Spot the Ball

Nowadays, it's easy for anyone with a computer and a graphics programme to open up a photo image and 'miraculously' make Great Aunt Dottie disappear, or even change the colour of their shirt to red and white stripes, as they really meant it to be at the time.

In the dim and distant past, however, it seemed like witchcraft when the pools companies – Littlewoods, Vernons, Zetters – took a snap of some hot First Division football action and then sent it out to their customers without the ball appearing in the coupon picture.

Just for the record, the ball was there in reality; it had just been expertly airbrushed out as surely as a pubic hair belonging to a naked volleyball lady in a *Health & Efficiency* magazine.

Now all punters had to do was to locate the ball's exact original position with a Biro 'X', stump up 20p and collect their cool £125K. The idea was to check the given weather conditions,

the score and the date, then follow the players' forlorn gazes and make an expert stab.

But those in the know bought one of these automatic multi-X rubber stamp gadgets, which made winning seem so inevitable it felt like cheating.

No wonder we never even got a sniff of a Marina 1300 Estate bonus prize.

ITV Sunday Afternoon Football

Who can ever forget the theme tune to Tyne-Tees TV's legendary *Shoot* on a Sunday afternoon? It was the sound that signalled the end of Sunday dinner and the start of a feast of TV football – one of only two possible sources available at the time, which made it so much more special than today's overload.

The Sunday dinner that had taken Mum hours to cook was wolfed down in two minutes. Roast beef and Yorkshire puddings lay in our stomachs, barely chewed, as we rushed to turn on the old black-and-white telly to warm up in time for that blasting fanfare, played over a backdrop of clips from games featuring the Northeast clubs...

Ba ba-ba-ba ba-ba BAH BAH BAH...

That's how the theme tune went. An archetypal 1960s

blast of a military band with a high-tempo oompah beat. The kind of tune that would only ever be used as a TV theme tune or as a novelty cha-cha-cha football single for a Cup finalist. In other words, pretty darn special.

Likewise the presenter, the great Kenneth Wolstenholme, forever famed for his commentary climax to the 1966 World Cup final.

But, best of all, we had a much better chance of appearing on the ITV show than on the BBC's national *Match of the Day*. We were on three-way rotation with Boro and Newcastle – not forgetting Darlington and Hartlepool, once a season if they were lucky!

The Birmingham Cheque

Sunderland were in the doldrums in December 1976. Hoping that a new manager might give them a boost, they took a chance on appointing Jimmy Adamson, the ex-Burnley boss.

Adamson's first game was at Birmingham City. The Lads slumped to a 2-0 defeat in front of a crowd of 24,597. The result left them joint bottom of Division One (now the Premier League) with West Ham.

It's hard to imagine that things could get worse but they did. The Lads scored in only one of their next eleven games and that was an FA Cup tie against Third Division Wrexham. A late-season resurgence almost rescued us but the famous shenanigans from Jimmy Hill when Coventry and Bristol City engineered a draw in the last game of the season thwarted Sunderland's great escape.

But, to get to the point, football was not the lucrative business it is today. Sunderland's share of the St Andrew's

gate receipts was a paltry £2,891.70. The Bank of England inflation calculator tells us that this is the equivalent of around £19,530 at today's prices. Put another way, the price of a three-year-old secondhand Qashqai.

There was no electronic transfer of funds in those days. So due credit to the Blues for posting the payment to the Northeast before Christmas. Let's hope it didn't get caught up in the Christmas post.

'Football's Foreign Legion'

These days the majority of Premier League sides are made up mainly of players born outside of the British Isles. But there was a time, not so very long ago, that the prospect of an overseas player coming to England was front-page news.

The first really big signings from abroad were the Argentinians Ossie Ardiles and Ricky Villa who joined Spurs in 1978 after both had featured in Argentina's World Cup win that year.

Sunderland decided to follow suit in December 1979 when they broke their transfer record fee by spending £380,000 to buy Claudio Marangoni from San Lorenzo. Manager Ken Knighton boasted that he had signed a quality player who would prove to be as good as Ardiles and Villa.

Twelve months and only 20 appearances later, chairman Tom Cowie complained that, "He might as well leave. He is being paid a stack load of money for playing in our reserves. Another example of economic lunacy." It has to be said that Cowie was not the world's greatest motivator, nor did his outburst exhibit much faith in the judgement of his manager, Ken Knighton.

Marangoni duly returned to Argentina and Sunderland saved themselves £150,000, having only paid £230,000 of the original fee. Inevitably, given Cowie's public views on him, Knighton was sacked in April 1981.

What became of Marangoni? Did he fade into obscurity, scarred by his tempestuous experience of playing for Sunderland? No, after returning to his home country he

shone for several club sides, winning medals galore and represented the national team nine times. So perhaps Knighton was a good judge of a footballer after all? Claudio just didn't do it for us.

Match Weekly

Looking back at the mind-blowing 1979 arrival of *Match Weekly*, the fanfare of fuss kicked up by editor Melvyn Bagnall seems slightly tinged with irony. "Our object is simple... to improve on anything currently available," Mel trumpeted... but we can't help thinking the original launch deadline was a bit earlier than 6 September – three weeks after the 1979/80 season's big kick-off!

At last, publishers EMAP were challenging the virtually unopposed market dominance of IPC and *Shoot!* And in eye-catching style, too, with a mag featuring more colour pages printed right to the edge, making *Shoot*'s white borders suddenly look very *passé*.

Inside there was a stellar line-up of writers: Keegan, Clough, Ardiles, Coppell, Atkinson and Jimmy Hill. Instead of 'Focus On' there was 'Match Makers', with loads more questions. Plus groundbreaking player stats. And a

free Transimage sticker album, too, with the first issue.

We jumped ship in droves, and now feel guilty; disloyal because the circulation war was a triumph of new over old.

Corinthians Mad!

Even hardcore Corinthian collectors won't recognise these super-rare Sunderland figures, and may well be turning green with envy at the sight of them.

On the back of the FAPL Collection blister packs for the 1996/97 range, releases for newly promoted Sunderland, Derby and Leicester were flagged up as 'coming soon in 1997'. But we're still waiting.

Luckily for us, Craig Robinson, author of the amazing *Football Crazy, Corinthians Mad!*, has these *unreleased* figures of Michael Gray, Tony Coton, Niall Quinn and Paul Bracewell among his 10,000 strong supercollection!

Album of the Year

What was the greatest LP released in 1973? If you are/were a bit of a rocker, you might go for Led Zeppelin's *Houses of the Holy*, or Bowie's *Aladdin Sane*. Mike Oldfield's *Tubular Bells* was huge at the time, as

SUNDERLAND'S CUP!
OFFICIAL souvenir record album of the
1973 F.A. CUP FINAL

MATCH COMMENTARY HIGHLIGHTS by arrangement with BBC RADIO ENTERPRISES

was *Wombling Songs*. Nah. There's only one correct answer, and there's little doubt that you still play it most nights. Here's the classic guitar/bass/drums/synth/vocals combo…

The Half-Time Scoreboard

Sunderland went many years without changing the format of their programme. From the 1950s until 1963 it comprised 12 pages and cost 4d, apart from 1958/59 when the board obviously decided that the blow of relegation to the Second Division would be softened if they reduced the price to 3d.

There was very little narrative in these programmes but they did contain one essential piece of information. The secret code for the half-time scoreboard. It sounds like a piece of ancient history now but when the half-time whistle blew all eyes turned to the scoreboard. We are not talking electronic or digital here.

The 'operator' would clamber up a set of ladders and take his position on the scoreboard gantry. If knowledge is indeed power, he was the most powerful man in the ground. He knew all the half-time scores.

The board had the letters A-P permanently affixed. The operator's job was to slide what looked like two large Scrabble pieces against each of the letters. Starting with 'A' he would insert a number denoting how many goals, if any, the home team had scored. Then we waited for the away team's number of goals. Looking back, it was quite exciting, a bit like awaiting a VAR decision. Tension was greatest when Newcastle's score was due to be revealed. If the home team (Sunderland and Newcastle hardly ever played at home on the same day) was shown as having scored two goals a cheer would go up followed by a gasp and a kicking of the ground when the Magpies earned a great big three. In desperation we hoped the operator was joking; but he

never joked. He took his duties very seriously. He was a smooth operator.

There were three 'sittings.' The scores for the first set of letters from A to P were shown for a couple of minutes then removed to be replaced by the scores of clubs from the lower leagues.

The whole process was not without controversy or the occasional argument. You only knew which match corresponded with each letter if you had splashed out 4d on a programme. Anyone found to be looking over the shoulder of a programme holder was likely to get at the very least a dirty look as the holder gripped the treasured half-time score code more tightly to their chest.

HALF-TIME SCOREBOARD		
No. 1	No. 2	No. 3
A BURNLEY / ARSENAL	A NORWICH / MILLWALL	A ROTHERHAM / HULL
B EVERTON / NOTT'M F.	B PLYMOUTH / CARLISLE	B BURY / TRANMERE
C FULHAM / LIVERPOOL	C PORTSMOUTH / BLACKPOOL	C OLDHAM / SWINDON
D LEEDS / STOKE	D PRESTON / BRISTOL C.	D CHEST'FIELD / HARTLEPOOLS
E LEICESTER / COVENTRY	E Q.P.R. / IPSWICH	E DARLINGTON / YORK
F MAN. UTD. / WEST BROM.	F BARROW / BRIGHTON	F WORKINGTON / BRENTFORD
G SHEFF. WED. / MAN. CITY	G BOURN'M'TH / THE ORIENT	G
H TOTTENHAM / NEWCASTLE	H BRISTOL R. / SHREWSBURY	H
J WEST HAM / SHEFF. UTD.	J COLCHESTER / NORTH'PTON	J
K WOLVES / SOUTH'PTON	K MANSFIELD / GILLINGHAM	K
L ASTON VILLA / HUDD'FIELD	L OXFORD UTD. / STOCKPORT CO.	L
M CARDIFF / BLACKBURN	M PETERBORO. / WALSALL	M
N CHARLTON / BIRMINGHAM	N SOUTHPORT / TORQUAY	N
P CRYSTAL P. / BOLTON	P WATFORD / GRIMSBY	P
R DERBY / MIDDLESBRO.	R ALDERSHOT / ROCHDALE	R

Given how rubbish Wi-Fi reception can be at most grounds, perhaps now would be a good time to bring back the good old half-time scoreboard? We're sure the operator would welcome his chance to rejoin the profession.

The Most Famous Mackem?

Many famous people have been born in Sunderland, from Emili Sandé to James Bolam and Terry Deary. Then there's James Herriot (real name Jim Wight), Alan Price, Dave Stewart (ex-Eurythmics), Kate Adie, Bob Willis and the Venerable Bede, to name but nine.

None of those named have, to date, appeared on the face of a Royal Mail postage stamp. A Mackem who has had that honour is Hendon-born Raich Carter, one of the greatest players ever to wear the famous red and white and clearly a contender for the mantle of the most famous Mackem in history.

In March 2022 Raich appeared on a set of stamps designed to celebrate the 150th anniversary of the first FA Cup final.

Royal Mail stamps relating to football were not unusual. For example, in 1996, a set called 'A Celebration of Football' was issued featuring players such as Dixie Dean, Duncan Edwards and Billy Wright.

2006 saw the release of stamps featuring Bobby Moore.

Also on every stamp was, of course, the head of the late Queen. She was not keen on sharing any stamp with a footballer or indeed, anyone else. In the mid 1960s, while he was Postmaster General, Tony Benn fought a battle

ROYAL PATRONAGE
King George VI and Queen Elizabeth present the Cup to Sunderland captain Raich Carter after his team's victory at Wembley in 1937.

FA CUP 150 YEARS

to create more commemorative stamps. One stumbling block was the Queen's head dominating too much space on the stamp. Ideally Benn, a staunch republican, would have removed the head altogether (probably literally!) but a compromise was reached and the size was reduced, creating more space for the likes of Raich.

The trouble with producing so many commemorative stamps is that you run out of things that justify commemorating. I suspect even Tony Benn would be shocked to see the list of topics featuring on Royal Mail stamps in 2025. They included 'The Vicar of Dibley,' 'AC/DC' and 'Monty Python'!

The Queen would not be amused.

Esso FA Cup Coins - and the Near Miss

It might seem a little bit greedy in retrospect, but as a mad-keen collector/hoarder of all things Sunderland, I did harbour just one secret regret following our incredible feat of winning the FA Cup back in 1973.

If only, I thought to myself, we'd managed to win the Cup *just one year earlier*, then we'd have been one of the teams featured on the big, gold, super-special commemorative coin that was only minted after the centenary final had been played.

Frankly, the honour seemed a bit wasted on Leeds and Arsenal.

Even so, good old Esso.

Every year, they brought out something great for

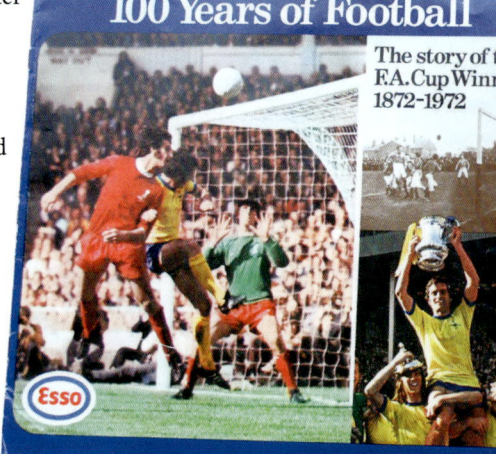

us to collect, and 1972's handsome FA Cup Centenary brochure and coin collection was such a must-have item for every young boy that silence must surely have descended on the forecourts of rival garages while the offer was on, with tumbleweed blowing around between deserted BP, Shell and Cleveland pumps.

There were 30 of these 'silver-bright, superbly-minted Centenary Coins' to collect, one per visit to the Esso station, the album to house them representing a modest Dad Tax of 15p.

As it is, Sunderland were still featured, the back of the coin recording our single FA Cup win to date, in 1937. But everyone from the Wanderers and Blackburn Olympic was very nicely trumped by that gold-coloured centrepiece coin. And it could have been us!

Protest!

Sunderland fans are renowned for their loyalty, and any protests are usually of the milder variety reflecting the calm nature of your average Mackem. In March 1995, the Supporters Action For Change Group decided they had suffered quite enough failure and had 12,000 'red cards' printed for the home game against Stoke City on 11th March. These were handed out to fans at the turnstiles. Fans making up the 12,282 attendance were asked to hold their cards up for exactly one minute at 3.10pm in order to "show their anger at what is happening at the club."

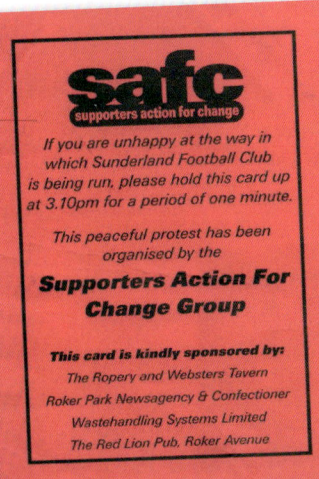

And that was the end of the protest.

Sunderland won the game 1-0 through a late goal by Andy Melville. I wonder what would have happened had they scored between the 10th and 11th minute? Would the crowd have refused to celebrate in much the same way a returning player often suppresses his delight when he scores against a former club?

The red card had no lasting impact on or off the pitch and Sunderland lost their next four games leading to the sacking of manager Mick Buxton who was replaced, initially on a temporary basis, by Peter Reid.

Reidy's team lost only one of their last seven games and relegation was avoided. There then followed three seasons of almost unbridled success, so the red cards were not seen again until 1999.

I don't know what it is about 10 minutes that stirs up protest? Perhaps 10 minutes into the game is when the last stragglers roll in from the pub? Whatever, on 3rd April 1999 Sunderland fans were once again asked to raise a red card in silent protest. This time it was against the threatened closure of Vaux brewery and the loss of up to 650 jobs.

Vaux had had a presence in the city since 1806 and were the club's shirt sponsors for much of the 1980s and 1990s. I don't know how many in the crowd of 41,135 held up their red card but it was all to no avail, as Vaux still went out of business.

However, in 2019, a Sunderland-based company announced their intention to resurrect the Vaux brand. Fans can now enjoy a pint of one of the many excellent beers and lagers produced by the new-born company before heading off to the Stadium.

Nike Make Their Debut

Even at the time it seemed like a groundbreaking deal when the American trainer manufacturer Nike selected Sunderland as the guinea pig for their first foray into the British football shirt market.

Let's not forget, it was only in 1979 that the company had supplied its first ever kit to any professional sports team – their own local team, the Portland Timbers, in the short-lived North American Soccer League. So we really were in on the ground floor of the massive worldwide expansion to provide shirts for thousands of different teams across countless sports. And once again it was down to a local connection, the Nike British HQ having been set up just down the road in Washington the year before.

Most importantly, it was an attractive and popular shirt, getting back to traditional stripes (albeit with white sleeves) after Le Coq Sportif's previous experiment with a whiter base. Decent sponsors, too, in Cowie's for two seasons, followed by Vaux in 1985/86.

Just one talking point, and that was the somewhat naive

move by the American designers to switch the conventional placement of the team crest and manufacturer logo, placing the Nike 'Swoosh' in what is traditionally thought of as badge-kissing territory!

The TV Gantry

They don't make 'em like this any more. When it came to old-school, traditional designs and values, there were few TV gantries in the English leagues that could compare with the magnificent example atop the Clock Stand roof at Roker Park.

Originally added in 1966 to provide space and facilities for the international media crowding into town for the four World Cup matches, you can rest assured any exotic commentators, cameramen and technicians weren't

pampered by the amenities, which were as basic as you could possibly get.

The Roker gantry was refreshingly chilly, wide open to the wind and rain, with access to hot drinks, food and toilet facilities only available via a walkway under the stand roof. Comforts were few and far between for visiting TV types: if they were lucky, the commentators might be afforded the use of a chair to help ease their attacks of vertigo, peeping straight down at the touchline half a mile below.

Compared to the luxurious, warm, waitress-pampered

indoor facilities at the Stadium of Light and every other modern stadium, the Roker gantry was TV Hell.

You thought the classic Subbuteo TV Tower was basic? Gah. That frozen '00'-Scale cameraman only had 15 feet to fall...

The Stadium of Light Takes Shape

In November 1995 when chairman Bob (now Sir Bob) Murray received planning permission to erect a new stadium on the site of the former Wearmouth Colliery he may have thought that was one big hurdle overcome. However, the local MP objected, claiming the new ground would cause congestion and the site should be used for leisure, housing, and light industry developments. Others jumped on the anti-new ground bandwagon and even Newcastle chairman Sir John Hall poked his nose in.

Luckily for the future of Sunderland AFC, Bob didn't give up and the Environment Secretary John Gummer rejected calls for a public enquiry. This allowed building work to commence in May 1996 on what was at that time planned to be a 40,040 all-seater stadium.

It was amazing to watch the stadium being erected and, looking back, difficult to imagine that what is now one of the best grounds in the world was once a building site and before that a coal mine.

The new ground needed a name, of course, and at midnight on 30th July 1997, just hours before the opening game against Ajax, the Stadium of Light was named. A lot of fans didn't like it initially, but there's no pleasing some people. Would they prefer something soulless like Everton's Hill Dickinson Stadium?

The opening event went well, with the crowd of over 40,000 experiencing only a few minor glitches and generally being awestruck by the new stadium. At the time, it hardly seemed random at all when vintage rockers Status Quo arrived by helicopter and the match ball was delivered by the Red Devils Parachute Team.

The night ended with a spectacular extravaganza of pyrotechnics – the first of many fireworks to come at the Stadium of Light.

As for the friendly game against the Dutch giants, that ended in a relatively unspectacular scoreless draw, but the night was all about the beginning of a new era, not a football match.

Avec

Here's another kit manufacturer that Sunderland chose to join with for their debut venture into the English leagues. British-based Avec produced a smart, traditionally striped kit for 1994/95, which left us

with great memories in its second season when promotion was won back to the Premier League. The first Avec kit came with two notable design flashes, namely an all-red panel on the left shoulder and a red and white striped addition to the

IN THE HEAT OF THE PREMIERSHIP

front of the black shorts – unique details which were then both dropped for a plainer shirt in 1996/97. Avec's away kits were something of a mixed bag: the unexpected 'teal' and red colours in 1994/95... whose shorts featured a

strangely unforgettable pattern of red stripes which seemed to make a target out of every player's groin area; a bright yellow strip with blue shoulder flashes in 1995/96; followed by a classy plain white shirt that was essentially the home kit with the red stripes removed.

Can I Have Your Autograph, Mister?

In the Brave New World of 21st-century football, there's no such thing as an autograph any more, the hasty scribble on the back of a fag packet having been consigned to the evolutionary dustbin by the selfie snapped on a mobile phone.

Also long since disappeared is the autograph book, that curious little volume with nothing inside but plain pastel pages of pink, green, blue and yellow. Always with the spine running down the short side!

And what about the crowd of small boys who used to hang around the locked double door marked PLAYERS AND OFFICIALS ONLY an hour after the match? It's all cordoned off now, out of bounds to mere fans. The players with the most sought-after scrawls have gone missing, too: men who didn't need a minder at their side to talk to a twelve-year-old about the afternoon's brawls and cannonballs. The kind of players whose personally signed message you'd want to treasure forever.

Real Roy of the Rovers Stuff

One of the greatest feelings available to any young whippersnapper in the '70s and '80s came on the scandalously rare occasion that Sunderland featured on the cover of their Saturday-morning comic.

For one week only, thanks to *Scorcher & Score*, the club's single FA Cup victory would be the focus of a whole nation's youth, young Dave Watson taking his place in the cartoon universe alongside Billy Dane (the kid with two left feet whose Victorian boots enabled him to play like Dennis Tueart) and Nipper Lawrence (the dirt-poor kid from the northern docks of

Blackport, drawn in authentic sooty style to signify his triumph over squalor).

In 1978, Sunderland goalie Barry Siddall must surely have drawn inspiration from *Roy of the Rovers* comic and 'The Boy in the Velvet Mask': Alan Hemmings was the son of a one-

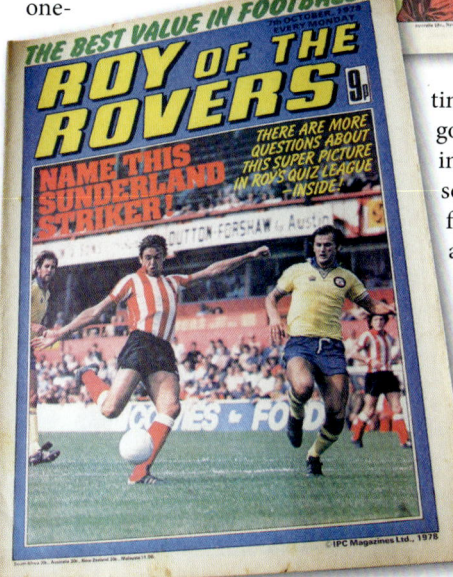

time England goalie paralysed in the line of duty, so forbidden from having anything to do with football. It wasn't enough to stop our hero donning a superhero mask and turning out for Lynchester United.

Clubcall

Back in the '80s and '90s, it was the sheer unavailability of up-to-the-minute club information that made it so valuable. You wouldn't want to miss what 'Wantaway' Peter Davenport had allegedly denied this morning – or boss Terry Butcher's counter-denials of any new midfield ace rumours. Ahh, the rumours…

The Clubcall service came as a blessing for all fans – especially those exiled from local news and those trapped at work with a free phone to avoid the disgraceful premium call rates.

At the end of the line – literally – was a local newspaper stringer summing up back-page stories from yesterday's evening paper and this morning's tabs. To deliver value for money, he also used to make up juicy filler on the spot, and read it out. S-l-o-w-l-y.

"Hello… and it's a big… welcome… to your exclusive… front-line… Clubcall service for… Sunderland… Association… Football… Club.

"Listen to… Clubcall… for all the latest… news… and… information…"

Because we were paying by the second.

Panini

As if it weren't enough for Italy and the Italians to have a natural superiority in the fields of fashion, history, weather, food, football tactics, motor racing and Claudia Cardinale, we then discovered that, all along, they'd also held an effortless advantage in the arena of football collectables.

True to form, we only found out about their magnificent sticker albums 17 years after Giuseppe and Benito Panini had first changed the lives of Italian kids; but we got there eventually, in 1978.

For years, we'd been quite content with our *Wonderful World of Soccer Stars* albums made by FKS, but when Panini's *Football 78* collection hit the newsagents, they were blown out of the water.

Our new favourite thing was twice as hefty as its predecessor, weighing in at a fat 64 pages; each club spread over two pages instead of one, with a grand total of 525 stickers to collect. Panini's unique selling point was that these 'stickers' were actually sticky, not just pieces of paper that required the use of glue. Unable to afford a Pritt stick, my experiments with flour and water had produced messy results in previous years. But now you could swap your stickers and seal them immediately in their allotted square.

The stickers themselves were beautifully designed, clear head-and-shoulders shots with a club badge and a St. George or St. Andrew's flag because, yes, the Scots had been included too. The English Second Division was also covered with a teamgroup and badge for each previously ignored team. Ah, how your heartbeat jumped when you ripped open your packet and saw a gold foil badge nestling among your half-dozen stickers!

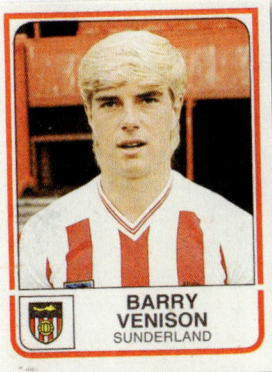

Football League Review

In an age when the good old football programme is seemingly in terminal decline, it's amazing to look back at the sheer popularity of the humble match-day magazine – which no one on the planet ever called it. Not only was the *Roker Review* a no-brainer buy, it also had the free *Football League Review* magazine stapled inside its covers. Whether you wanted it or not!

The mag was run from Football League secretary Alan Hardaker's Blackpool bungalow, devoted to showing what a big, happy family their 92-member club was. It shouted proudly about the popularity of the League Cup, which added greatly to the League's visibility vs that of their old enemies at the FA – hence the *Review*'s conspicuous absence from certain larger League grounds.

The only real downside came when some lazy programme editors merely added a bare minimum of their own content on either side of the supplement!

The *Review* was 5 pence 'when bought separately', which is to say never. It was full of behind-the-scenes peeks at the day-to-day running of all the League clubs, an article on the bootroom at Barrow being just as likely as a visit to

the Arsenal trophy room. Its allure was almost entirely down to staff photographer Peter Robinson, arguably the greatest of them all, who spent whole seasons travelling around snapping mascots at Mansfield and tea-ladies in Tranmere, thinking up ever more unusual formations for his teamgroups. Robinson never missed an oddity or a location, showing more interest in football culture than the game itself. He went on to work for FIFA and shoot World Cups up to 1994, before being controversially frozen out of the Premier League action.

Airfix Footballers

By the time the '70s rolled around, the postwar fervour for playground WW2 battles, DIY Airfix models and gun-toting comic heroes was slowly starting to subside. As kids, our only knowledge of Desert Rats and Hampden bombers came from movies, mostly old and black-and-white. So what a thrill to discover the equally paintable football figures first released to surf the wave of soccermania after the 1966 World Cup.

At last, a chance for boys with a steady hand, infinite patience and a single-hair brush to paint our 1/32nd scale Airfix Footballers in authentic colours – red and white, of course – and maybe also a few of the other traditional football colours that somehow seemed more exciting than khaki and grey.

Jeepers Keepers!

Yes, it's true to say that our coverage of Avec's admirably classical, traditional contribution to Sunderland's kit history – just a few pages back – did draw a discreet veil over the manufacturer's less modest moments. And no, we're not just talking about that jaunty striped patch on the shorts.

We are talking an op-art psychedelic explosion of bad taste in a paint factory. With big fumbly goalie gloves drawn on the bottom. Ouch!

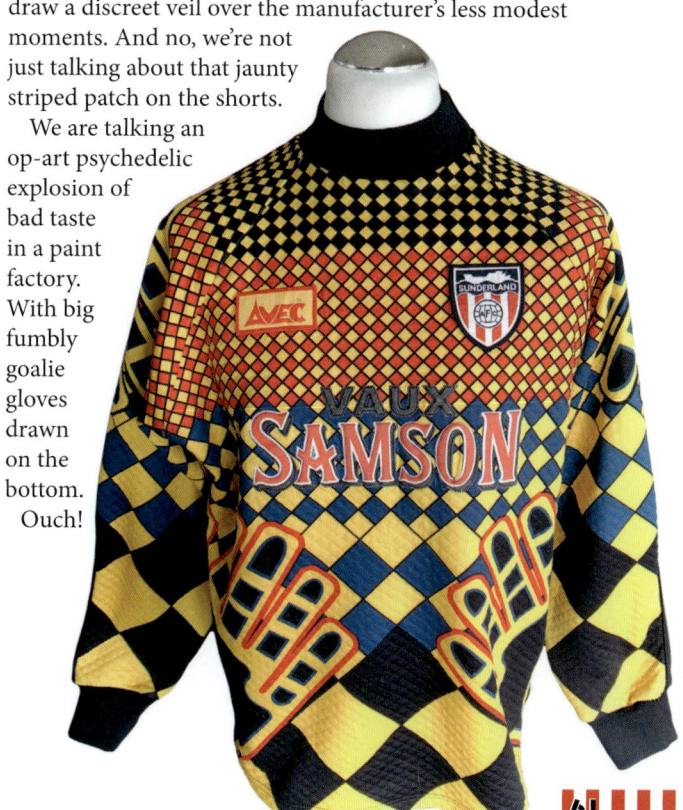

Goal Magazine

They called it 'The World's Greatest Soccer Weekly', and right from the off in sunny 1968 *Goal* magazine did always have an optimistic, stylish look wrapped around its weekly complement of (almost up-to-date)

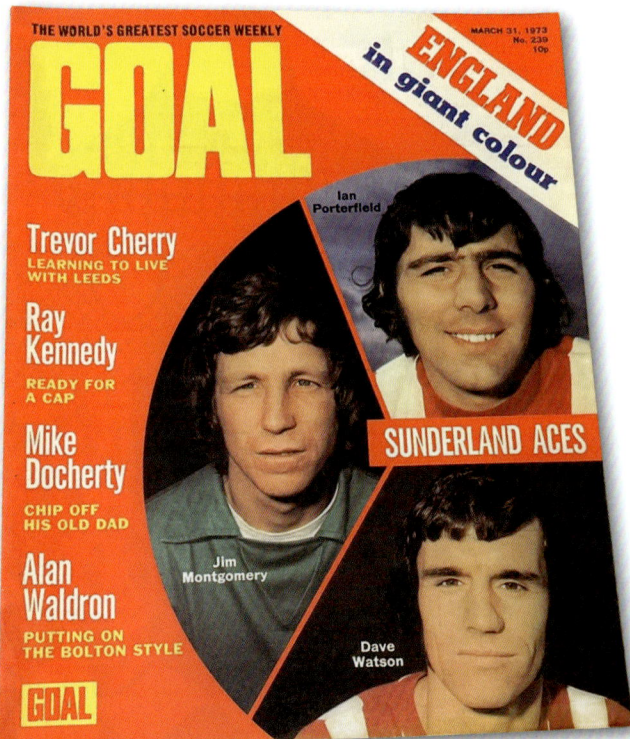

news, (big) opinions and (frankly flimsy) features.

The mag's distinctive covers, with a bright yellow title on a red background and circular photo design, owed a nod to mod and to pop art. It was between the Technicolor covers that the slight problem arose: a distinct lack of Sunderland content! We'd make our loyal weekly purchase in the hope of a Sunderland player's glam missus appearing in 'Girl Behind the Man', some behind-the-scenes SAFC insights in 'Terrace Talk', or a kind word in the Billy Bremner column. A 'Flashback' or a made-up reader's letter in 'Goal Lines', maybe?

On the positive side, if you flick through a large pile of copies from 1969 to 1974, when *Goal* was killed off – sorry, 'incorporated into *Shoot!*' – you will find a full-page black-and-white pic of Billy Hughes in white boots (he 'could be a key man for the Roker Park club when they start their bid for promotion'); a half-page pic of Dave Watson; and a match report vs Vasas Budapest: 'Sunderland were quite impressive.' Aww, thanks for that!

Paint Jobs

It's a crime against football, against art and an individual player's human rights. And all for the sake of filthy lucre, and international capitalism's relentless march toward profit. There aren't many things in life that can cause as much alarm as a hastily recoloured kit on a football card or sticker.

There's a creeping sense of injustice as you spot the evidence of iffy airbrushing that can leave you feeling somewhat soiled.

And at the heart of the scandal lies our own Mick Docherty, whose very name on cards was often wrongly given as 'Mike'.

To add insult to injury, in 1973 Mick was on the wrong end of a dodgy A&BC paint job that saw his old Burnley kit lazily overlaid with our stripes. And he'd played

for Man City in the interim!

Four years later, the cheapskates were at it again, painting a childish red collar on a 'Sunderland' kit – in a picture clearly taken at the Burnley training ground. It makes the rubbish 1976 touch-up of Pop Robson's West Ham kit, complete with fake creases and shadows, look like the work of Leonardo da Vinci.

And so to the FKS Soccer Stars album for 1977/78, and a further crushing revelation: there's only one thing worse than crap paint jobs, and that's when they don't even bother and leave Mick in his old City kit!

Put Your Shirt On It

Gambling is such a big part of football, yet if a player should fancy a flutter a lengthy ban can ensue.

Almost all clubs have a raffle with the winning numbers being selected at half-time by a former player,

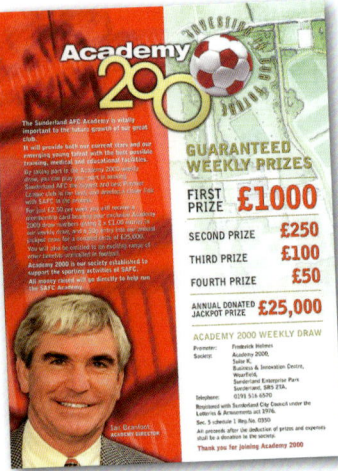

preferably one who has turned out for both the home side and the opposition. Or by David Speedie if you fancy the chance to antogonise the away supporters.

Sunderland took the raffle concept one step further by introducing 'Academy 2000', which was a weekly draw paid by direct debit. The jackpot, even 25 years ago, was a whacking £25,000.

The quirkiest competition was the 'Roker Goal Time.' For a mere 5p you could buy a sealed ticket which, when peeled open, revealed your 'match time.' If by some miracle the first or last goal came within five seconds of your match time you could win £30 for the first goal or £10 for the last goal.

This led to some perverse behaviour. Rather than trying to cheer the ball into the net, you were pleading with the Lads not to score until your goal time beckoned – at which point you urged them on as if your life depended on it.

If you'd drawn a time such as 89 minutes 10 seconds and

THIS IS YOUR MATCH TIME:

Min. **Sec.**
69 **53**

Voucher to be produced whole when claiming Prize Money Guaranteed
Torn or mutilated tickets not accepted

the match was goalless going into the last few minutes, you didn't really care who scored, the temptation of a £30 prize outweighed the disappointment of a possible 1-0 defeat!

Another short-lived venture was a 'guess the size of the crowd' competition. It was geared around Sunderland's brief sojourn in the European Cup Winners Cup and called 'Into Europe With The Team', hence the lack of longevity. Showing immense optimism, I opted for a crowd of 38,985 for the first game of the 1973/74 season against Orient. The actual crowd was 28,211 – not even close!

Fixed-odds coupons have now pretty much taken over the football betting industry, and are widely available online, in betting shops and around the stadium. But they'll never match the hopeful anticipation of opening a 'Roker Goal Time' ticket...

Shoot!

I can remember my first *Shoot!* as if it were yesterday: the day I finally graduated from cartoon strips to hard news, from fantasy to a heavily edited, schoolboy-friendly version of the facts. Allowed one comic a week, I'd already moved on from the entry-level *Beano* to the mixed sport and action papers such as *The Victor,* but not until 1970 did I consider myself man enough to step up to *Shoot!*

Eight pence was the price of admission to absorb words of wisdom written by Bobby Moore, and to puzzle over the fiendish problems posed in 'You Are the Ref'. There was a wealth of World Cup live action accompanied by stats and hard-luck stories; but it was reading the 'Goal Lines' letters page and 'Ask the Expert' readers' queries that I first felt a sense of community, realising there were football-mad kids just like me all over the country.

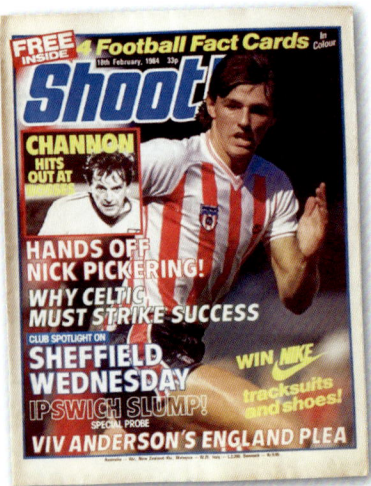

Shoot's 'Focus On' Q&A proved a lasting icon: it's still referred to by men of a certain age with regard to favourite food, alternative employment opportunities and '70s motor cars that seemed snazzy at the time. And then there were the teamgroups and single-page posters that allowed you to fill your bedroom wall with pictures of your heroes.

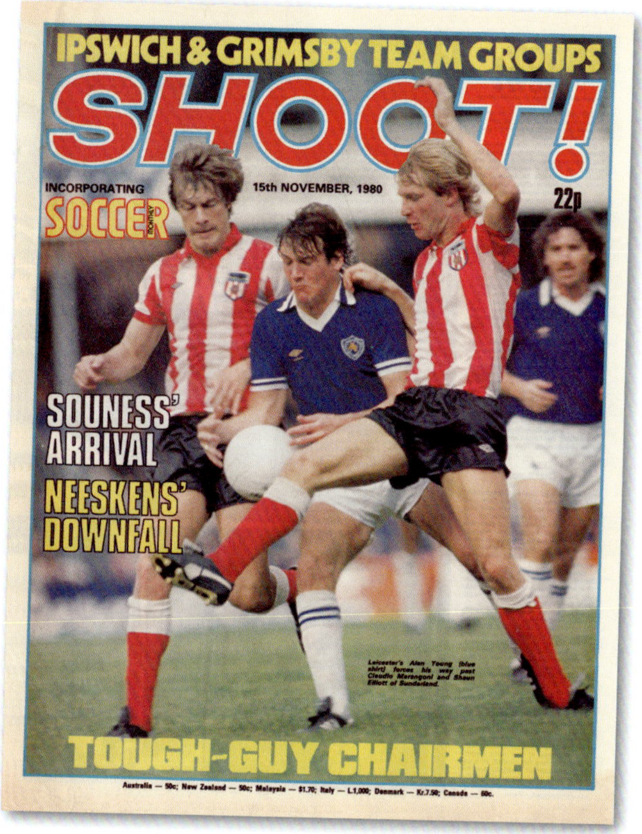

But it was *Shoot*'s small-ads that really fuelled my football fantasies. Football watches and caps, tracksuits and trainers to die for. Supersoccer magnetic football. Garden Goals...

Scarf Ace

The best thing about that immortal design classic, the two-colour bar scarf, was that it marked you out not only as a 'dyed in the wool' football fan but also as a follower of your particular team. It was a real rite of passage, to get your first red and white stripy scarf for your birthday around junior-school age – lovingly knitted by your mam or by good old gran – first to wear proudly to school, and then to your first match. It was the epitome of class, wearing your scarf neatly tucked into your V-neck jumper or coat, or tied around your wrist.

But then came a new evolution in the story of the stripy scarf. The introduction of a third colour, a touch of black, helped separate Sunderland fans from, say, Liverpool fans (with their touch of yellow). But neither the old nor the new system worked so well when we played Boro, or Man United... hence the popularity of scarf embellishments such as enamel badges ('Sunderland Rule OK'), cloth patches ('Next to Ali, Sunderland Are The

Greatest') and stitching that spelled
out the names of favourite players.

The next evolution was the so-called
'silk' scarf, made from 100 per cent
polyester and clearly printed with block-capital club names
and slogans that finally left little room for doubt.

Until some idiot dreamed up the 'half-and-half' scarf.

Them Up the Road

I had been going to games at Roker Park for five years before my mam let me go to a game against Newcastle. It was 1970 and we drew 1-1 with a Bobby Park equaliser. Sadly, there was more action off the pitch. In the days before segregation and all-ticket matches, Sunderland and Newcastle fans clashed in the Fulwell End. Meat paste jars seemed to be the weapon of choice, and dozens

queued up to have a stitch or two inserted by the overworked St John's Ambulance people. Thankfully, crowd control has improved by leaps and bounds since then.

Derby games are horrible when you lose but nothing can beat the feeling of beating the Mags, and 20th-century memories benefit from an extra rose-tinted glow:

February 1979 – A 4-1 win at their place. Who can ever forget the Gary Rowell hat trick?

April 1980 – 1-0, special for me as it was the first time I'd seen us beat them live. I can still picture Stan Cummins swivelling and putting the ball in the net.

May 1990 Play-off semi-final 1st leg – a goalless draw, with Paul Hardyman missing a last-minute penalty then being sent off for trying to kick the Magpies' goalkeeper John Burridge in the head.

May 1990 Play-off semi-final 2nd leg – 2-0 win at St James' Park. A Geordie pitch invasion failed to get the game abandoned, and we were on our way to Wembley!

When I Owned SAFC

footballers often refer to "them upstairs." They mean, of course, the owners and directors. In the past it was usually a successful local businessman that owned or ran the club. Burnley had Bob Lord, a butcher. Louis Edwards at Manchester United was also in the meat trade. Manny Cousins of Leeds dealt in furniture. Sunderland had the Collings family whose main interest was laundry.

For many years young north-eastern talent would desert Sunderland and instead ply their trade at Turf Moor. Could it be that the offer of a weekly pork chop, a sirloin steak

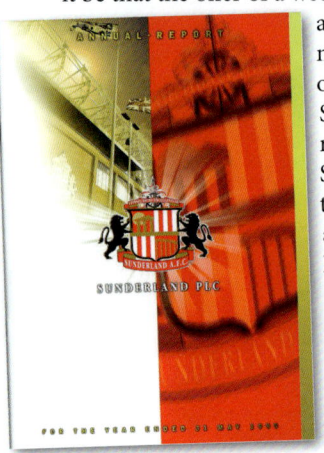

and a pound of sausages appealed more than a perfectly pressed pair of trousers? The advent of StaPrest trousers probably removed the only incentive Sunderland's higher echelon had to offer local young starlets such as Ralph Coates, Peter Noble and Ray Pointer.

In 1996 we all had the chance to go 'upstairs', or at least peer from the foot of the staircase. Shares in Sunderland AFC were put on the market and anyone could apply. Those with a few bob to spare received a shiny new share certificate and, every six months, alternately received an annual report and interim report full of figures and long, accountant-type words.

Then in 2006 along came Drumaville Limited, the Irish

Dear Former Shareholder,

It has now been a while since the takeover of the Club in July 2006 and the compulsory purchase of shares from holders

I know the purchase of the Club was an emotive issue for many supporters, with some reluctant to sell their shares and unhappy with the compulsory purchase. I do hope you understand that our reasons were valid and with the best interests of the Club and its supporters at its heart.

The Club had always planned to return the certificates to all former shareholders, unfortunately this process has taken much longer than anticipated for some.

Please find enclosed your certificate returned as a souvenir and, where appropriate, a cheque relating to your proceeds from the sale of the Club.

I would like to take this opportunity to thank you personally for your continued support, it is greatly appreciated.

Kind regards.

Yours sincerely,

**Niall Quinn
Chairman**

consortium that compulsorily purchased the club, including my 200 shares. Niall Quinn did send me a very nice letter thanking me for the small part I'd played in the running of the club, and hoping that I'd understand that my removal from the stairwell was taken "with the best interests of the Club and its supporters at its heart." I think he was probably right; but for 10 years I did enjoy owning a little bit of Sunderland AFC.

The Video Age

One of the most anticipated events each summer, along with the release of the fixture list and the publication of the *Rothman's Football Yearbook*, was the launch of the club video showing the highlights of the previous season.

Luckily, the Sunderland videos were usually worth the wait and in the football-free summer months fans were able to relive either an heroic escape from relegation or a barnstorming march towards promotion. The titles on the VHS boxes told it all, really: *Black Cats Top Dogs; Sunderland AFC Champions; Last Minute Heroes; Wear On Our Way*, and *On The Up.*

Which brings us neatly to the 1993/94 season. There was no promotion challenge or serious threat of relegation as Sunderland coasted to 12th place in what is now the Championship. They won 19 games and lost the same number. Only five teams scored less than their pathetic haul of 54 League goals; meanwhile, a stingy defence conceded only three goals more than were scored.

This one was going to be hard

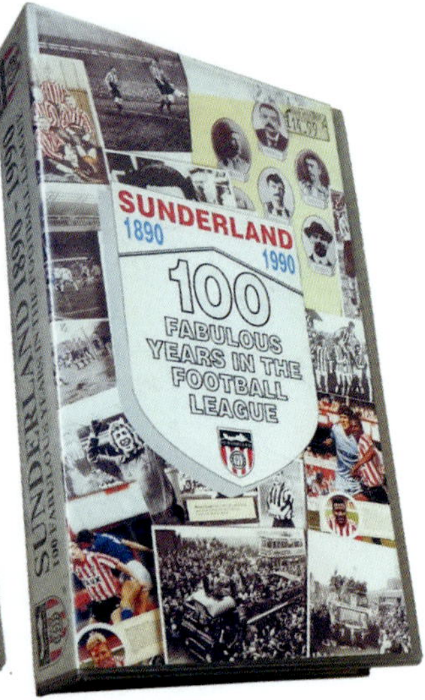

to sell. *Fifty Greatest Corners*, perhaps? But there was no guarantee that 50 could be found, and describing any as 'great' could attract the attention of Trading Standards. *Fifty Greatest Throw-Ins* didn't quite have the ring of a best-seller. In the end, pragmatism won the day with the agreed title, *Sunderland AFC 93-94*.

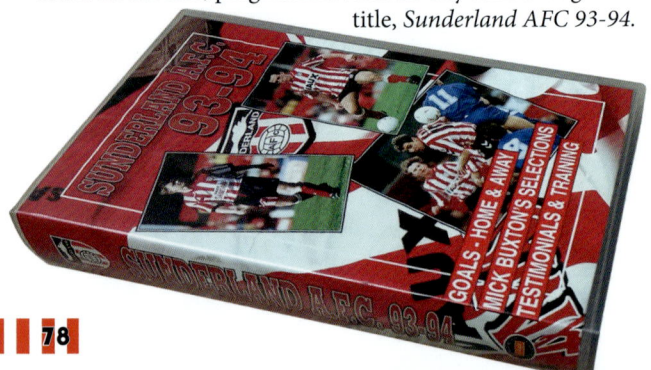

If that wasn't enough to entice the Mackems to buy a copy, they were promised 'Mick Buxton's Selections' and 'Testimonials and Training.' Buxton is a nice man and top coach but he isn't the world's most inspirational orator. In fairness, Churchill at his peak couldn't have roused the viewer into thinking the 1993/94 season hadn't been so boring after all.

Buxton lost his job in March 1995 to be replaced by Peter Reid. Despite escaping relegation by the skin of their teeth and being the lowest scorers in the Championship, the mood was much more upbeat leading to the release of *Reid's Revival – All The Goals; All The Action,* described on the video cover as "An all in all exciting video for everyone interested in the great Reid Revival." It certainly beat watching Sunderland players training.

Programmes - the '60s

Ever since the 1950s the programme's content had remained pretty much unaltered, with very little narrative and the same old cover featuring an overhead photo of Roker Park and the old club crest.

Suddenly in 1963 it was reduced to a pocket version; but despite the smaller size, the number of pages only increased to 16. Then, for 1966/67, the programme had a total revamp. The front cover showed the newly built club entrance plus an action photo which changed for every game. The price, which had been 6d since 1963, jumped to 9d. But the content remained resolutely much as it had been for the previous ten years.

The next price increase came along in the 1968/69 season with the programme now setting you back by 1 shilling. Included as an insert was the *Football League Review,* described as 'The Official Journal of the Football League'. What does stand out is the number of adverts for cigarettes and tobacco. The Roker End sold hot dogs, hamburgers and ice-cream while the Fulwell and Roker Cafés rather pretentiously offered toasted sandwiches and smorgasbord. I guess the latter was pitched at fans with European qualification in mind!

In 1969 we gained a title, *Roker Review*, along with a new cover showing an action photo and the team line-ups and officials. The programme was now much chattier, including a spotlight on one of the players and the 'Alan Brown Page.'

Manager Brown was clearly a man under pressure. His column, in the style of Donald Trump, breaks into block capitals when bemoaning the negativity around the Club: 'THIS MEANS

THAT WE WILL NOT TOLERATE SLACKERS… OR MEN WHO ARE NOT PREPARED TO RUN THEIR HEARTS OUT FOR SUNDERLAND.'

However, it seems his message missed the intended target, as the Lads were relegated at the end of the season.

Programmes - the '70s

The Sunderland programme kept the *Roker Review* title throughout the 1970s but quadrupled in price during that time and had several changes of format.

Starting the season at 1 shilling a copy, the first change came in 1971 as a result of decimalisation, when one old bob became five new pee. This really messed up the peanut man's hollering of "peanuts, tanner a bag, peanuts." A tanner used to be sixpence, but '2½p' just didn't have the same ring to it.

In 1972/73 there was a modest price rise of 1 pence. We had an extra four *Roker Reviews* that year because of the FA Cup run, and the most expensive programme of the season was the 15 pence we laid out for the FA Cup final against Leeds.

Perhaps capitalising on the feelgood factor of Wembley 1973, the club increased the price of the *Roker Review* to 10 pence in 1973/74. The

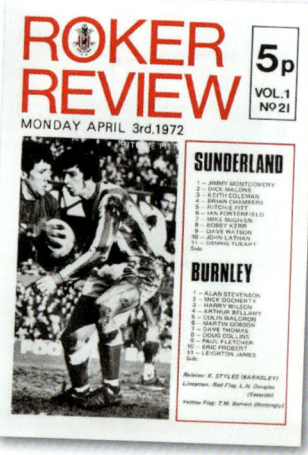

programme for the New Year's Day 1974 game against Notts County celebrated Monty's 500th game, and controversially pondered whether the League should be expanded from four to five divisions.

The only major change in the 1974/75 season was

the addition of 'The Matchday Magazine' after *Roker Review*. The title grew even longer the following year when

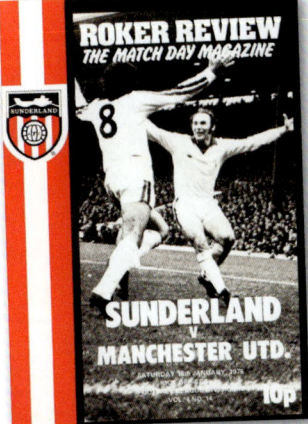

'Official Programme' was also added. The 'Lucky Face' competition was still going strong, with five crisp £1 notes going to a lucky person who had been

photographed at a previous home game.

A 50 per cent increase to 15 pence, a change to landscape and an action photo covering the entire front cover were the big changes for 1975/76, the team line-ups being relegated to the final page. The cover boasted of 'Features by Doug Weatherall and

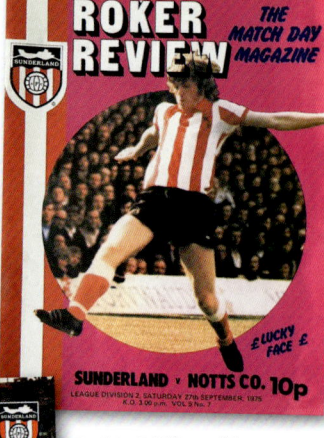

Jackie Milburn' but didn't say who the opposition was!

1977/78 was comfortably the best programme of the decade both in terms of cover design and cover content: the candid, informal and fan-friendly photos taken behind the scenes and in the stands were like a flash-forward nearly 20 years to the groundbreaking *Premier Passions*.

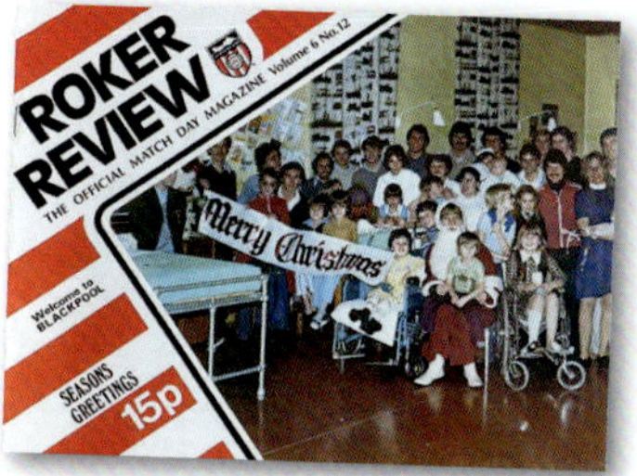

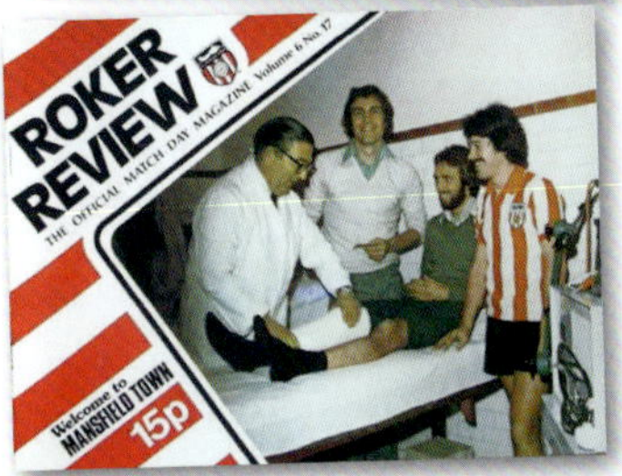

The full set of covers form a brilliantly clear and honest story of the season, with so much atmosphere

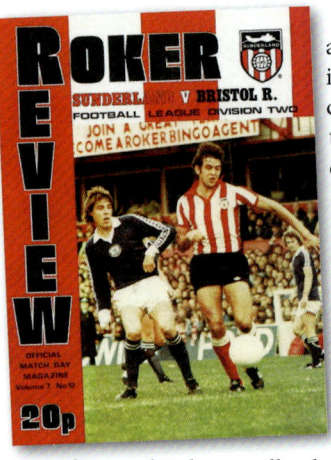

and detail captured in every image: the scarf-wearing queues and crowds waiting to get in the turnstiles in the days before replica shirts; the girls in the crowd; the players' treatment room and a weight training session.

Best of all, these programmes gave ordinary fans the chance to appear on the cover of their own club's official publication, restoring the balance between the star professionals who usually play for the club for a few years before moving on, and the spectators who pay their money to watch the games decade in, decade out.

So, all in all, it was a bit of a disappointment to immediately slip back to not-very-exciting match action for the end of the '70s. Again, the teams weren't listed on the front cover of the *Roker Review* but at least our opponents were named. No date, mind. But yes, we did notice the price notch up rather quickly from 15p to 20p and then 25p!

Programmes - the '80s

It wasn't just at Sunderland but across the whole Football League where the dawn of the 1980s marked a strangely unstable era in the design of the football programme. And just in case a dizzying sense of trial and error wasn't enough, there was another price hike too, to 30p.

Yes, the '80s did have the odd oasis of bold design style. It was the decade of *i-D* magazine and *The Face*, but football programmes were far less certain in their direction, which led to a complete redesign and a wildly different style almost every season!

Maybe it was a case of new technology coming in, and designers being inspired to show off all the zing and pizzazz and ker-pow of their new boxes of tricks. It certainly kept us fans on our toes, wondering which combination

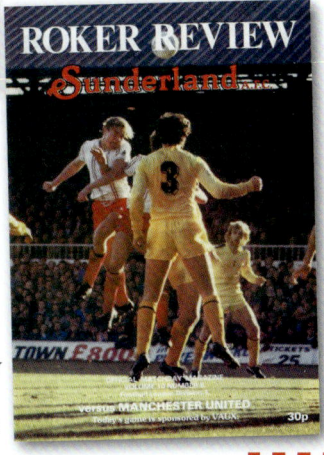

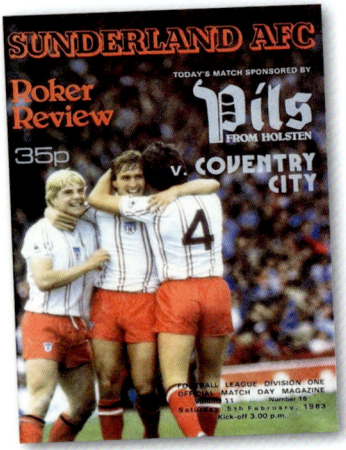

of groovy fonts, coloured frames, sponsor info and smallprint would be thrown together into the pot.

Quite interestingly, the *Roker Review* ceased to be for a couple of years mid decade, when the unfussily titled *Sunderland AFC* took its place.

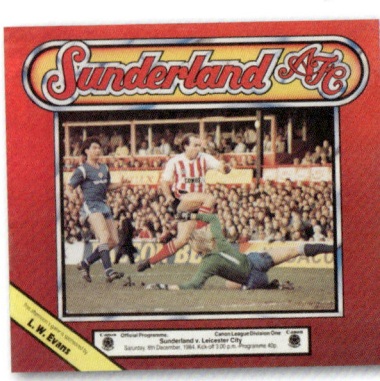

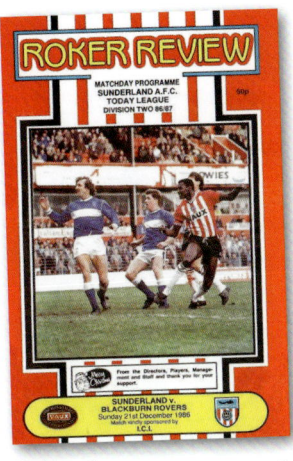

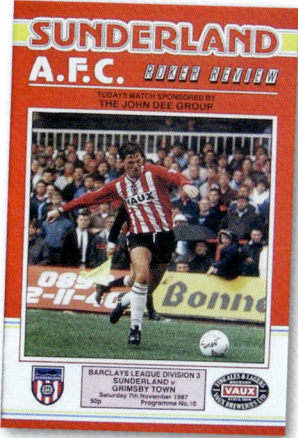

Relax, there was no cause for overdue concern. By the end of the '80s the *Roker Review* was back – yay – in smart new red and white (and yellow and blue) trim, though now its price had vaulted to 50p.

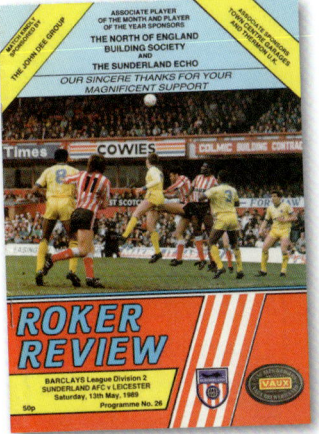

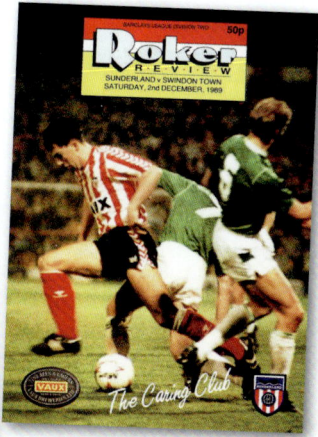

Programmes - the '90s

Back in the 1960s and '70s it was possible to buy yourself a smart plastic folder from the club shop in which to collect and store your programmes for a whole season. You see them up on eBay every so often, a whole year's history of changing team selections (with Biro amendments!), news and views and awayday images from the previous weekend presented in a volume no bigger than a fairly chunky book. You

could fit a whole decade's worth on a bookshelf with plenty of room left over for your collection of Sunderland AFC mugs.

But then, in the '90s, with the birth of the Premier League, the old club programme was transformed into an ever thicker, ever glossier affair. There was certainly plenty to read at half-time, but now you struggled to get the matchday magazine into your back pocket, never mind a season's worth into a single folder. It was time to get your

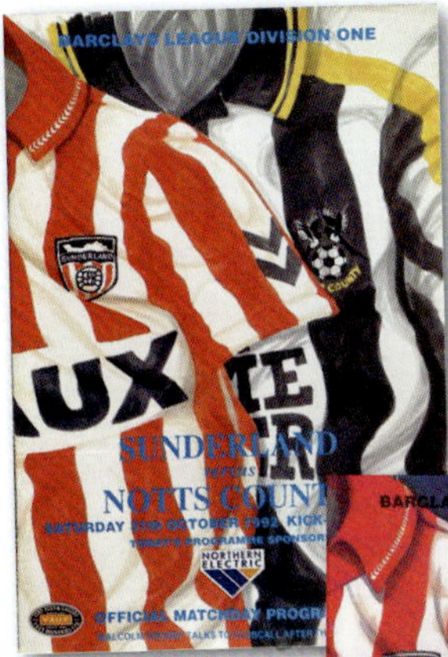
BARCLAYS LEAGUE DIVISION ONE
SUNDERLAND
versus
NORTHERN ELECTRIC

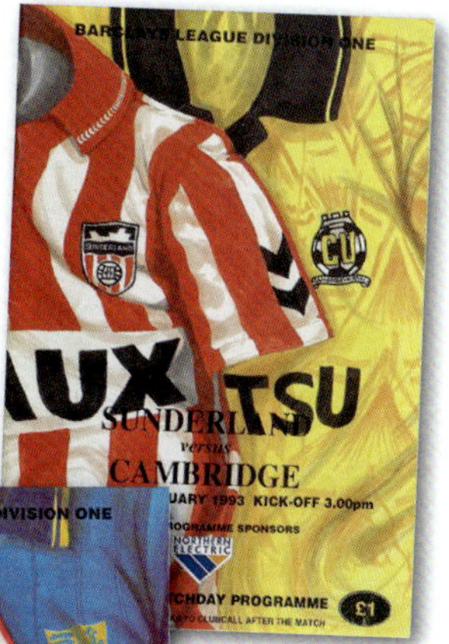
versus
CAMBRIDGE
£1

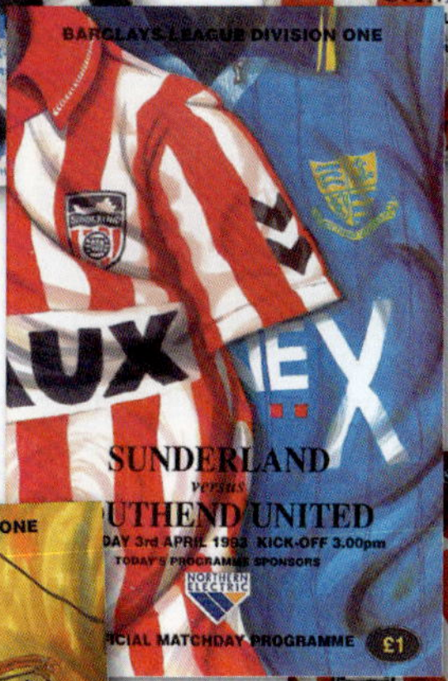
BARCLAYS LEAGUE DIVISION ONE
SUNDERLAND
versus
TODAY'S PROGRAMME SPONSORS
NORTHERN ELECTRIC
£1

BARCLAYS LEAGUE DIVISION ONE
SUNDERLAND
versus
WOLVERHAMPTON WANDERERS
TUESDAY 3rd NOVEMBER 1992 KICK-OFF 7.45pm
TONIGHT'S PROGRAMME SPONSORS
NORTHERN ELECTRIC
OFFICIAL MATCHDAY PROGRAMME
£1
MALCOLM CROSBY TALKS TO CLUBCALL AFTER THE MATCH

SUNDERLAND
versus
CHARLTON ATHLETIC
NORTHERN ELECTRIC
£1

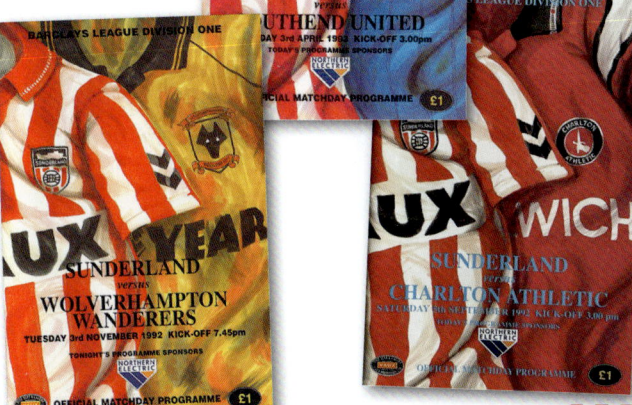

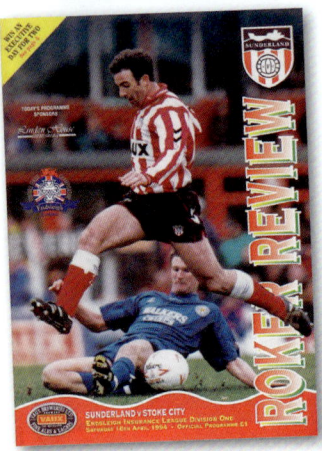
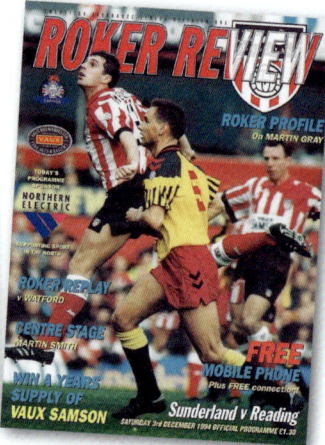

bookshelves strengthened to bear the weight of the weekly tonnage being produced.

Some of the new fonts on offer were pretty exciting stuff,

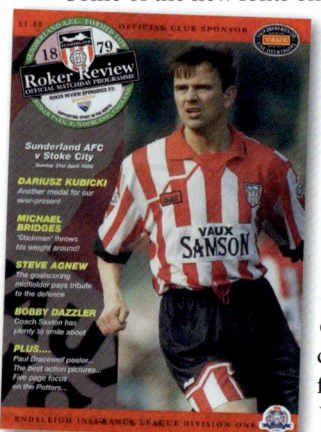

all fuzzy and 3-D, and mixed up on the cover in dynamic modern fashion, crowded around telephoto-lens images of players in action.

One exception was the '92/93 season which had some pleasing artwork of the Sunderland and opposition shirts.

The real benchmark of evolution came at the end of the decade, with the name change from *Roker Review* to *Red 'n' White Review*. Not too many

grumbles were heard about this decision, for obvious reasons. Eyebrows were raised, though, when the price first doubled to £1 at the start of the decade, then again to £2 by its end.

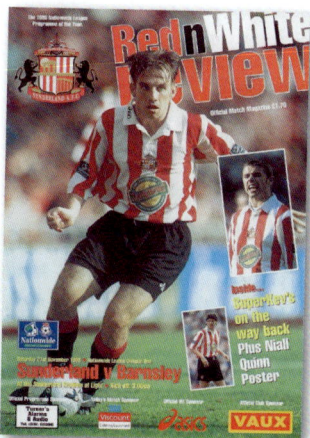 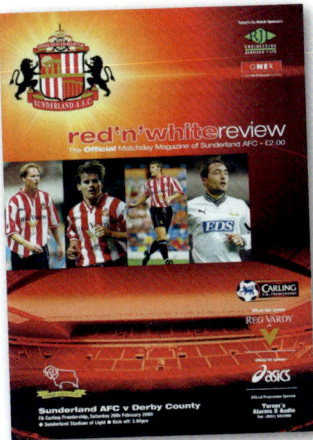

Flick for Kicks

Just like it was back in the day, there are two distinct types of Subbuteo fans and aficionados: first, there's the Player, who just wants to get his hallowed green blanket smoothed out on the carpet and get down to business flicking and kicking to win; and then there's the Collector, for whom the game itself is a bit 'fiddly', fun to play for a while, but hardly the main attraction in the '00'-scale universe dominated by dreams of those hypnotically desirable green boxes and their contents.

When it comes to nostalgic memories of childhood, the Player tears up readily at rose-tinted fantasies of retrieving well-flicked players from under the settee, of bending free-kicks into the top corner with his sidespin technique from just inside the 'shooting zone' that everyone else

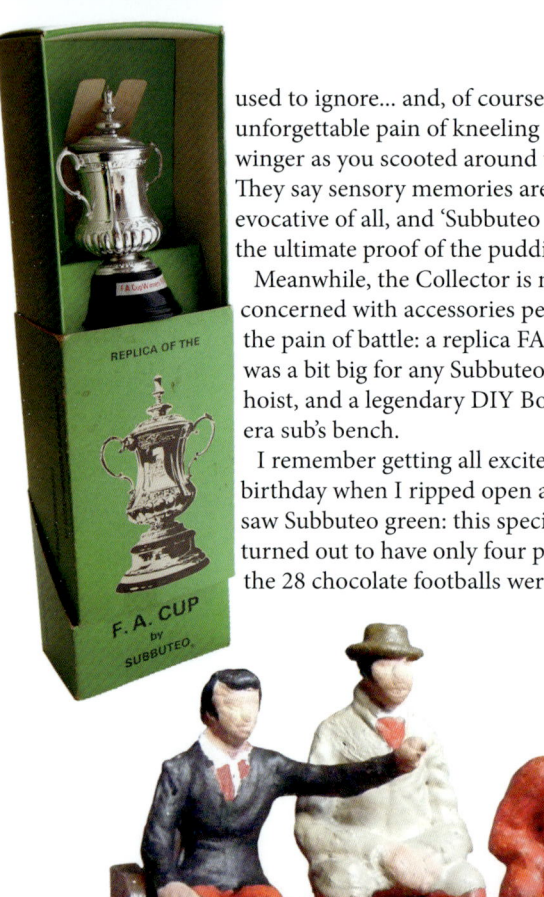

used to ignore... and, of course, the sweet, unforgettable pain of kneeling on your left winger as you scooted around the carpet. They say sensory memories are the most evocative of all, and 'Subbuteo kneecap' is the ultimate proof of the pudding.

Meanwhile, the Collector is more concerned with accessories peripheral to the pain of battle: a replica FA Cup that was a bit big for any Subbuteo player to hoist, and a legendary DIY Bob Stokoe-era sub's bench.

I remember getting all excited one birthday when I ripped open a parcel and saw Subbuteo green: this special gift set turned out to have only four players, but the 28 chocolate footballs were delicious.

1973 and All That

The story starts on Friday 4th May 1973. Looking back, I should have been at school but my focus was very much on preparing for the big day. I thought it would be sensible to try and get some sleep in the afternoon but there was no chance of that. My mind was racing. "This time tomorrow…" was my recurring thought.

Me and my three mates, Barrie, Paul and Kelly, were booked on the midnight train to King's Cross. Was it coincidence that Gladys Knight released 'Midnight Train to Georgia' just three months later?

We met at my house and then walked the mile or so into town. Everyone along the way wanted to shake our hand and wish us luck. It was as if we were heroes going off to war. I expect the fact that most people were drunk at that time on a Friday night was also a factor.

Barrie's mam owned a pie shop, and we were carrying loads (and I mean loads!) of pies, pasties and chicken legs. Once in the train carriage we were happy to share our goodies, so if any of you can remember the lads on the train dishing out chicken legs – that was us.

It was very quiet when we got to London so we decided to go and see Tottenham's ground which, logic told me, must be in or near Tottenham Court Road. After walking for an hour or two we gave up. It would be several years before I finally got to White Hart Lane.

Panic struck when I reached Wembley. My £1 standing ticket was in a different tier to my three mates. I begged the turnstile operator to let me through, and he relented. I guess it didn't unbalance the stadium too much to have one 16-year-old in the wrong part of the ground. Thank goodness it wasn't all-seater.

Pre-match 'community singing', as it was known, was provided by Frankie 'Mr Moonlight' Vaughan, but only after half an hour of music from the Combined Bands of the Scots and Welsh Guards and, bizarrely, two athletics events and a display by the Ayr Majorettes.

Folks at home would be enjoying watching *Cup Final It's A Knockout* while we showed total disinterest in the pre-match entertainment. The press the following day declared, unsurprisingly, that there was "little enthusiasm" for the athletics which saw Dave Herron win the 800 metres and Belgian Emiel Puttemans finish 50 yards ahead of Britain's Dave Bedford in the 3,000 metres. The match itself will always be remembered for Ian Porterfield's goal, Monty's double save and Bob Stokoe's dash across the pitch at full-time to embrace his heroic keeper.

Ironically, I now live in Leeds and when I tell Leeds supporters that I'm a Sunderland fan, they invariably bring up 1973 and tell me how lucky we were. Many of them were not even born in 1973! I tell them to watch the DVD of the game or read the newspaper reports from the days that followed. No one but no one claimed Leeds were unlucky at the time. The stats showed that Sunderland had 20 shots and Leeds had just one more, while David Harvey made more saves than Monty. Living up to their reputation as 'Dirty Leeds', the Yorkshire side committed 21 fouls compared to Sunderland's mere 13.

I'm not pretending that the last half hour didn't seem to last forever but undoubtedly the best team won.

After the match we hung around the entrance. Sir Alf Ramsey came out and we shouted, "What about Watson and Monty for England now?" He gave a smirk. I wonder if Dave Watson knows we were responsible for getting him into the England team?

Eventually we returned to the centre of

London to catch the midnight train to Sunderland. There was no crowd trouble. Indeed, the Leeds fans tried to console themselves by singing 'we'll keep the cup up north.' Clutching at straws...

It was light when we got back to Sunderland. We'd gone well over 24 hours without sleep. After sharing a few memories of the game with my mam and dad I went off to bed; but only after they solemnly promised to wake me in time to watch *Shoot* at 2.15pm.

It's hard to believe nowadays, in the internet age, but when I watched Porterfield's goal on TV that Sunday afternoon, it was the first time I'd seen it since 3.31pm, live in Wembley Stadium the previous afternoon.

It was exactly as I remembered it, and it will remain imprinted on my brain forever – along with that miraculous double save, of course.

The Wonderful World of Soccer Stars

It seems bizarre that no one in Britain had the idea of producing football stickers until after the wake-up call of the 1966 World Cup – this despite these obsession-inducing collectables enjoying huge popularity for decades on the Continent and in South America.

Cigarette and A&BC cards, yes; stickers, no.

Finally, FKS came up with the perfect formula in their *Wonderful World of Soccer Stars* albums, cleverly opting to produce football stickers without any hint of actual stickiness. Cue a million albums ruined by fumbly fingers trying to 'apply adhesive here' along the top of the stickers' backs.

Another stroke of genius was to use almost exclusively black-and-white photos – then choosing to amateurishly add in a layer of their own garish, inaccurate colour using felt pens and airbrushes. That's how they managed to get that authentic late '60s look of a crowd that was all black and white with a pinkish sepia tint.

Anyone who collected these so-called stickers in their childhood will recognise the recurring images that cropped up over the years in successive albums: the strangely familiar kids who got lucky with a tunnel-side spot when the FKS snapper was in town; other youngsters standing down below pitch

It's SUNDERLAND — 1973 F.A. Cup W

level at the front of the stands, with no advertising hoardings to hamper their view; and randomly recoloured opposition

333 TREVOR SWINBURNE

326 MEL HOLDEN

players from indeterminate teams.

Then, in 1973, something unprecedented happened that made every Sunderland kid feel like we'd won the football pools. For the first and last time ever, FKS honoured a Wembley triumph with a special two-page album slot. The curious stickers featured the tension of the Sunderland bench, the lads bouncing on the hallowed turf with the Cup, and Micky Horswill leaning on his sticker frame so he could reach out into your living room. That's FKS magic for you!

All this and some ground-breaking clipart, too...

Leitch's Fascia

The undisputed leader in football architecture in the first half of the 20th century was Archibald Leitch. As the popularity of association football rocketed, the Glaswegian was the man to call when you needed to add a few thousand to your ground's capacity.

His trademark flourish was the steelwork lattice fronting the top tier of his grandstands. This feature could be seen at footballing cathedrals like Ibrox and Goodison, and then Roker Park got one of its own. Leitch's Main Stand was opened in September 1929, costing the princely sum of £25,000. For their money Sunderland got 5,875 seats

positioned grandly above a terrace that held 14,000.

By the time Sunderland upped sticks and moved to the Stadium of Light the stand had undergone a number of modifications to Leitch's original vision. Red plastic seats, including some in the lower tier, executive boxes and grey cladding on the roof. But the best alteration was painting the balcony steelwork red, over the original dark green.

And someone had the foresight to rescue a couple of sections and take them over to the Stadium of Light, where they have a new home in the car park. Thanks are due to whoever it was that decided to preserve this piece of our football and architectural history.

Anyone doubting that a length of riveted steel can have a place in the hearts of Sunderland fans should note the modern reproductions housed within the Stadium of Light

Hopefully, Archibald would approve.

Farewell to Roker Park

All good things must come to an end and, in 1997, we left our beloved Roker Park. Everyone has their favourite memories of the place. In terms of sheer exhilaration, mine would be the 1973 FA Cup fifth-round replay against Manchester City. In second place comes our 6-2 victory over an Alex Sabella-inspired Sheffield United when we scored twice in the last three minutes to give us the four-goal winning margin necessary to take us to the top of Division Two.

There were two 'final' games at Roker Park. The first was our last ever League game on 3rd May 1997. Not for the first time, we were battling to avoid relegation from Division One. Our opponents, Everton, were all

performance of the season, running out winners by three goals to nil.

The *Football Echo* headline read 'New Hope For Roker' but, spoiler alert, we lost eight days later at Wimbledon and dropped out of the Premier League.

That Everton game was watched by a capacity crowd of

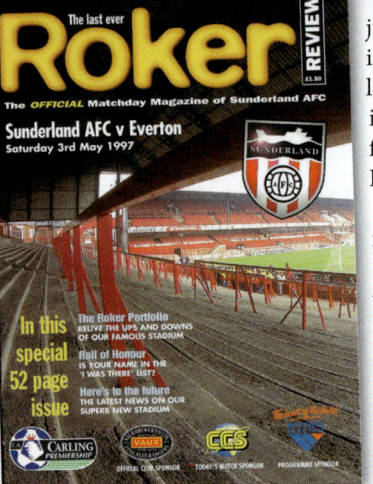

just 22,108, which sadly illustrated why we had to leave Roker, a ground that in 1933 had held 75,118 fans for a Cup tie against Derby County.

The more emotional final game was held on 13th May 1997 and was termed 'Farewell to Roker Park'. The opponents were Liverpool, a repeat of the first ever game at the ground in 1898.

The itinerary began at 6.20pm with a quiz and

Sunderland -v- Liverpool
Tuesday 13th May, 1997
K.O. 8.00pm

Itinerary for the evening:

6.20pm	Quiz and spot prize entertainment for supporters around the ground with The Metro Jets
6.30pm	Farewell to Roker Park Supporters Challenge Cup Final Darlington SAFCSA -v- John Laing Builders
7.00pm	The story of Roker Park commences with music and commentary from throughout the Club's history.
7.10pm	Junior Parade of Club Colours
7.15pm	Roker Legends Lap of honour commences
7.45pm	Story of Roker concludes
8.00pm	Sunderland -v- Liverpool
8.45pm	Announcement of the results of the Greatest Ever Match Poll Vaux Samson Band
9.00pm	Second half
9.45pm	Vaux Samson Band You'll Never Walk Alone/Abide With Me Removal of the centre spot by Charlie Hurley & Kevin Ball Final speech
10.00pm	Finale-Red and White Laser Show

ended with a red and white laser show almost four hours later. For 30 minutes before kick-off, a procession of 'Roker Legends' made a lap of honour. The game was secondary to all the memories and tributes, but Sunderland did win by a single goal, which was a repeat of the scoreline in 1898.

At 9.45pm the centre spot was removed by Charlie Hurley and Kevin Ball, and we all said our goodbyes to the ghosts of Roker past.

Diamonds Are Forever

Although Umbro had been making quality football kits since 1924, few fans appreciated the dominance of the Cheshire manufacturers. In the days before anyone was ostentatious enough to brazenly wear logos on the outside of clothes, Umbro confidently hid their light under a bushel, as God intended. Thus FA Cup, World Cup and European Cup glories passed anonymously.

So it came as quite a surprise when branding began to slowly creep in around 1973. The little diamond logo started to appear on shirts, and Sunderland were among the very first, along with Liverpool and Leeds... until, on the eve of the 1976/77 season, an advert appeared in *Shoot!* proclaiming: "It's going to be a sparkling season... just look at those diamonds!"

Bam! Six years after Brazil had won the 1970 World

Cup in plain Umbro shirts, the new range of kits now sported dozens of diamonds, with multi-logoed tape down the sleeves and shorts, just as Admiral and Adidas were rolling out similar branding. At the time it seemed outrageous; but Umbro's cutting edge was soon decorated with pinstripes,

334 TONY TOWERS

shadow stripes, button-down and lace-up Edwardian revival collars. There were reversible shirts, 'tailored' shirts and grey ones that 'looked good with jeans'...

The Black Cat

When Sunderland AFC held a public vote in 2000 and declared the nickname of 'the Black Cats' to be official, it left many fans – local and nationwide – slightly confused, as this was a name and image that had already long been associated with the club. So, what was the origin of our link to the lucky moggy, and why has it become so obscure over time?

As recently as 1972 club stationery featured an SAFC crest with a black cat balanced atop a football. The same image had served through the 1960s without ever appearing on a shirt. Earlier still, Sunderland fans had carried toy and inflatable cats to matches through most of the 20th century, the 1937 FA Cup win being famously attributed to the live mascot smuggled into Wembley by 12-year-old Billy Morris.

A black cat's head appeared on the programme cover in the '20s and '30s; and in the 1900s the chairman was drawn in a cartoon with one – and soon after, players were photographed with a 'lucky' black cat at Roker Park, where it was held to have halted a run of bad results.

But the origin of the name apparently goes back to the mid-18th-century Black Cat Gun Battery at the mouth of the River Wear, long since demolished but sited close by Horatio Street in Roker, where the club moved in 1883.

Mystery over. Up the Black Cats!

Going, Going, Gone...

In 1997 there can surely have been no Sunderland fans who had seen the team play their home games anywhere but at Roker Park, a stadium they moved to in 1898. Clubs don't move home very often, every 100 years seems about par for the course.

When Roker Park closed for business the contents were put up for auction. Turf, turnstiles, signs and tip-up seats, (perhaps a seat that had been occupied by the same season ticket holder for 50 or more years) were the sort of items you would expect to see in an auction. But a football ground consists of much more than a pitch and some seats to watch it from. The contents of manager Peter Reid's office, for instance, included a Zanussi refrigerator. Imagine boasting to your disbelieving friends that the fridge in your man cave once actually cheered up Peter Reid! The manager's office also offered a Philips 24-inch colour TV with Teletext. The bracket holding the TV to the wall was for sale separately, which does seem a little penny-pinching on the part of the club. After all, the stadium manager's TV came with the wall-mounting bracket included.

In a show of elitism, the directors' boardroom had a TV two inches bigger than Reidy's. Not only that, but it also had Teletext plus a video player. Presumably, if the manager wanted to watch upcoming opposition in action he had to wait for the directors to vacate the boardroom and slip his VHS into their machine.

The stadium manager was clearly the cutting-edge IT guru of Roker Park with his Dell 286 PC, a printer and two (yes, two!) computer tables.

I purchased a slice of turf at the auction, for old times' sake. After all this time I've forgotten where I put it on the lawn; but it doesn't really matter as the memories of those great, and sometimes not so great, times at Roker Park will live on forever – unlike a Zanussi refrigerator.

The Football Echo

finding out the football scores hasn't always been as easy as Googling 'BBC Football.' In the 1960s and '70s, if you missed the scores on the BBC teleprinter or the reading of the results on *Sports Report* at 5 o'clock, your next chance of finding out if your favourites had won came with the delivery of the *Football Echo*.

At quarter to six or so, a shopful of people would crowd into newsagents throughout the town. My nearest was Mary Fielder's in Hylton Road. The anticipation was intense. Then a van would pull up, very briefly, and the delivery man hurled a batch of papers into the shop doorway. Mrs Fielder, fully realising how important the content of this delivery was, cut the string around the precious package and laid the papers out on her counter to be devoured by eager readers wanting to see the scores, to check their pools or discover if their letter to the editor had been included that week.

You didn't have to look at the scoreline to know if

Sunderland had won, drawn or lost. The front page always featured a football with a man's face, two arms and two legs. If he was smiling and had his arms in the air, we had won. A slightly downbeat expression with hands on hips denoted a draw. A look of total misery meant we had lost.

Another visual indicator on the *Football Echo* was the colour of the paper. Up until Sunderland's first ever relegation in 1958 the paper was printed in pink. This partly denoted Sunderland's proud record of being the only club to have always played in the First Division. The shame of relegation turned the paper blue, and it remained that way until the club's first ever promotion in 1964 when the pink print returned.

The *Sunderland Echo* was another key part of footballing nostalgia. It was delivered every teatime (that is, about five o'clock in Sunderland – none of your posh 'evening meals'), and I can remember every Saturday looking at the stop press for the Lads' half-time score.

One sticks in my mind for some masochistic reason. It was 19th October 1968 and we'd been out collecting wood for a bonfire on Guy Fawkes' night. Bonfires were serious businesses in those days. We started collecting early and posted someone on guard to prevent raids from rival gangs. Looking down the stop press I was stunned to see West Ham FOUR v Sunderland NIL. It got worse, of course, and we ended up conceding eight – or '8 (EIGHT)' as the teleprinter showed it, just in case the viewers thought there had been some mistake.

Alas the *Football Echo* is no more. Modern technology means we can get the scores by pressing a few buttons on our phone. But no doubt in the future, scientists, professors and academics will marvel at how 20th-century man was able to produce an entire newspaper with scores from across Britain and get it onto Mary Fielder's front porch only one hour after the games finished. It seems like an unbelievable 'rose-tinted' memory but it really did happen.

Action Man

never mind Norman Bates out of *Psycho* with his dual personality problem, spending half of his life as his old mum up in the attic. Back in the Golden Age of Toys, Palitoy's Action Man had a far more alarming condition: one day he'd get all dressed up as a soldier, then he'd do a quick change to become an astronaut. A deep-sea diver. A Nazi. Even, occasionally, a footballer.

Sadly, he wasn't much good for football games because he was unable to stand or kick without the aid of a fragile plastic frame.

You might say he was a bit of a dabbler.

Still, he looked a million dollars in his chunky-knit Sunderland shirt your Mam knitted him for Christmas.

Premier Passions

nowadays a new fly-on-the-wall football documentary series is nothing special; we've seen it all before through the politely invasive eye of Netflix, the broadcaster of choice to promote the brand of clubs who

hope to sell more replica shirts across the globe.

But long before the likes of Manchester City, Spurs and Wrexham succeeded in boosting the celebrity of

their players, managers and owners, Sunderland were the groundbreaking guinea pigs.

Shot during the 1996/97 season after promotion from the second tier, *Premier Passions* was the first documentary series ever shot behind the scenes at a football club. And it made for compulsive viewing – especially if you weren't a Sunderland fan.

It was brutal. No-holds-barred. A warts-and-all window in on pure chaos.

Because the rules hadn't yet

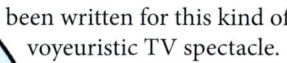

been written for this kind of voyeuristic TV spectacle.

The five 45-minute episodes were supposed to showcase 'a new beginning' (according to narrator, Gina 'Our Friends in the North' McKee) for a club and a team ready to step up and take on the best; but instead they provided a painful record of financial concerns and big decisions, injuries, a lack of goals, and a miserable slide back out of the Premier League under new national media star, Peter F****** Reid.

Widely acknowledged as the greatest soccerdoc ever made, it's nevertheless the model that other wannabe celebrity clubs strive to avoid.

Over the course of the filming, a safe mid-table place in mid season became a battle for survival, Reid and assistant Bobby Saxton effing and jeffing as they lost control, patience and finally the will to live.

The boss never did look like he was going to cheer up, never mind sign a new striker. "I don't know whether yer think I'm f***in' stupid but yer not givin' it to us. Back into

them. Get yer body there and make 'em kick yer. I'll tell you what, it has been poor. Don't look at me as if I'm f***in' daft. It has been poor. The most important thing on that pitch is that football..." Peter Reid was only 41 at the time, but ended up looking 71.

The move away from Roker was fast becoming reality, and the club's share price was a hot talking point in the directors' box; but some of the most memorable moments came courtesy of the four talking heads pulled from the diehard fanbase. Maybe we'd have fared better if they'd been in charge in the dressing room and boardroom...?

The Schoolgirl nails it in episode one: "I mean, 8 million's not a lot to set aside for players, and yet he's putting all this money aside for his new stadium. And I think he should concentrate on the team first, rather than the stadium and rather than floating Sunderland on the Stock Exchange."

The Painter-Decorator has got what it takes, celebrating a win by sneaking into the SOL building site and befriending the security guard lying in wait with his dog. "In my lifetime following Sunderland I've probably had more lows than highs; but the good times is coming. I think they are."

The Lab Technician provides sound tactical analysis: "To be perfectly honest, going to watch Sunderland you don't see a lot of skilful football, it's a lot of battling and guts."

"It's a nightmare," says the Bloke from the Chippy with one game to go. "To be honest, it doesn't feel reet. I've been nauseated, sick all day."

But it's SAFC fan Gina's voiceover in the penultimate episode that hits hardest of all: "Disappointment is something you can cope with; it's the lingering hope that really hurts…"

The 105-Point Season

The 15- and 19-point seasons were truly agonising times, but our points tally in 1998/99 almost made up for the misery we were destined to suffer in those two dreadful seasons.

In 1998/99 we scored more goals than any team in the Championship (91) and conceded the fewest. We lost only three games. If we went a goal down, absolutely no problem – we knew we'd score two or usually more. It was a sensation like flying, nothing could go wrong and nothing did. In the month of November we gained 15 points. That's as many as we would manage in the whole of the 2005/06 season.

Everyone loves a list, especially magazines, and in July 1999 *FourFourTwo* listed the top 50 players in each of the English divisions. In Division One Sunderland players took four of the top 10 positions,

and that didn't include Kevin Phillips who, inexplicably, came in at number 11. Ten Sunderland players made the top 50. No wonder we walked away with the title. The main absentee from the list was Nicky Summerbee which seems an aberration as he was responsible for dozens of pinpoint crosses that Niall Quinn either put into the net or nodded down for Super Kev to finish off.

It's perfectly possible that 105-point seasons only come along once in a lifetime or when, like Wayne Rooney's Birmingham City in 2025, you're relegated to a level where you can't help but win every week.

The season almost got even better. The League Cup, then a much more prestigious trophy than it is now, saw Sunderland reach the semi-final where they played Premier League Leicester City. Leicester had beaten three Premier League clubs to reach the semis whereas Sunderland had defeated only one, Everton at Goodison Park on penalties. That game was probably the latest I've ever been at a football ground – watching the regulation 90 minutes, half an hour extra-time and then 12 penalties.

The semi-final was played over two legs with Leicester deservedly triumphing by two goals to one at the Stadium of Light. The return leg at Filbert Street was a different matter, with Sunderland bombarding the Foxes' goal and going ahead through a Niall Quinn header. Sadly, Tony Cottee, who I once saw score four goals against us for Everton, netted an equaliser and Leicester got to Wembley where they lost out by the only goal of the game to Spurs.

'70s Prices

What would you give for a time machine that would allow you to go back to the Sunderland club shop in the '70s?

A twenty pound note, nowadays wiped out by a modest round in the pub, would enable you to fill your carrier bag to the brim with SAFC treasure.

Now let's see: a crimplene hat would look smart; and a belt; a pennant, large and small; a silk scarf, or two, one for each wrist; a Parker pen; a key ring with Bob Lee's face on it; an autograph book just in case; a pillow case, a teddy bear for your little brother; several badges...

IDEAL GIFTS FOR CHRISTMAS

Crimplene Hats	95p	Teddy Bears	2.95p
S.A.F.C. Belts	95p	Pillow Cases	1.85p
Players Photos key rings	50p	Watches - Ladies & Gents	9.95p
Pennants - large	55p	Parker Pens	1.95p
Pennants - Small	35p	Lighters	1.40p
Silk Scarves	85p	Club Scarves	1.95p
S.A.F.C. badges	95p		

Other gifts include: Torches, Metal Badges, Ashtrays, Brandy Flasks, Plaques, Autograph Books, Wallets, Sunderland Cup records, Tankards, Team and individual player colour photographs etc. etc.

SHOP OPEN AFTER THE GAME TODAY

SHOP HOURS:- Daily 9.15 a.m. to 5.30 p.m. (except Sunday)
Friday late shopping - 7.15 p.m.

Treasury Tags

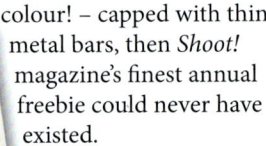

The humble treasury tag is one of those items of 20th-century stationery that has rather fallen out of fashion in the no-paper office and today's virtual, screen-based Brave New World. Bring back the paper clip, the stapler, and the lever arch file, we say. Not forgetting the vital hole punch, of course. But, first and foremost, let's hear some long overdue appreciation for the treasury tag.

Why? Because if it weren't for these short lengths of green string – never any other colour! – capped with thin metal bars, then *Shoot!* magazine's finest annual freebie could never have existed.

Year after year, we collected up the 13 consecutive issues – three whole month's worth – after the exciting arrival of the free cardboard cover. Borrowed the hole punch from dad's bureau where he kept his bills and fixture list. Stole two tags from the small packet stored next to his Sellotape dispenser. And lo! Finally, we could create our own brand-new book

from the folded pages, featuring
the Sunderland *Captain*, Sunderland's *Football Firsts*,
Sunderland's *Stars of Britain*, and *Shoot's Stars of the World
– 111 Great Internationals*.

Hmm, bit of a
rubbish year,
that last one.

Pre-history

Before that fateful, life-changing day when you very first strode in manly fashion through a vomitory and took in the sheer enormity, the sounds and smells and sights and mud and magic of Roker Park (or the Stadium of Light – whippersnapper!), it's no exaggeration to say that the real world of football never existed.

On a purely personal level, that is. Before that day of your debut, you knew virtually everything there was to know about football. You'd seen millions of pictures and videos, and had even been allowed to stay up late on Saturday night to watch *Match of the Day*. You knew the name of every

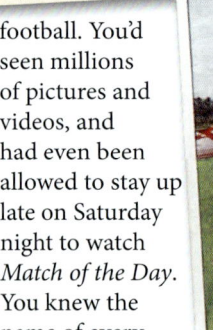

of every Sunderland player, as well as his middle name, previous clubs and What He Would Have Done If He Hadn't Been a Professional Footballer (assuming he'd been featured in a magazine Q&A).

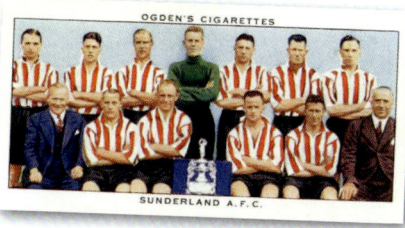

But now all of this peripheral, preparatory kids' stuff – the comics and the football cards/stickers, the football games played at carpet level or on screen, the TV pundits' expert analysis, the playground and park games in replica football shirts – finally snapped into perspective.

Football history started here. No matter whether we'd won the Cup the year before (and tragically you'd just missed out) or we'd had a miserable year in the third tier (and you'd been lucky to miss it), none of that stuff was really *real* to you. You weren't there. So, on that all-important personal level, it may as well have never happened.

Which is a bit of a strange feeling for Sunderland fans, especially – because when you look back at the club's

storied past and enviable honours list, it's probably true to say that the club's greatest days were all over by the 1950s, when we were known as 'the Bank of England Club'.

It's bad enough to have missed out on the 1998 Play-off final – a classic match, even if we did lose. But that disappointment quickly palls into insignificance compared to missing Sunderland coming second in the League in 1935, then winning it in 1936 and lifting the FA Cup in 1937.

Which in turn pales into insignificance up against the exploits of Sunderland's 'Team of All the Talents' who won the League title four times between 1892 and 1902, whilst also finishing as runners-up no less than three times.

It would have to

be said that back in the days when football was played in black-and-white between teams who moved in suspiciously jerky motion down the wings and in on goal, Sunderland were pretty bloody good. We even won the World Cup in 1895, an accomplishment that all of us modern-day fans still feel strangely proud of, even if our grandads weren't born at the time. Yep, we beat Scottish champions Heart of Midlothian in a match that was billed as an unofficial 'World Championship' decider.

Maybe we'll win it again next season, eh? And we'll all be able to watch pre-history repeat itself.

Topps of the Pops

The 1970s were a great time to be a youngster. We missed out on all the stress of the three-day week, inflation and the Cod War, and concentrated on the good things in life: long, hot summers spent up the park, great pop music and hundreds of Sunderland victories over the likes of Brazil and Newcastle – at Subbuteo.

It may seem strange to say now, but a huge amount of the colourful pop culture we gorged on at the time was founded on the American Dream of all-time great pop and disco 45s; classic rock albums, Hollywood

blockbusters and cult TV like *Starsky & Hutch* and *The Bionic Woman* (or was that just me?).

The new Admiral football kits were even bringing a gullwing-collared, multicoloured,

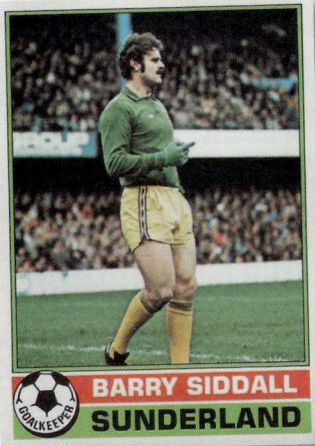
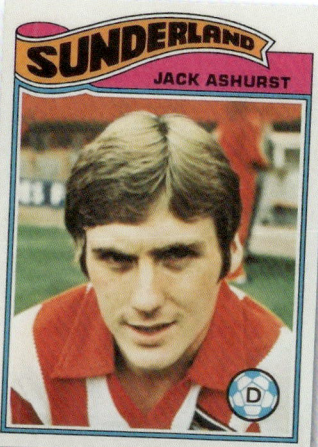

go-faster glam-rock superhero vibe to the football field. So what a thrill when football cards also took a sudden lurch in a mid-Atlantic direction.

When staid old A&BC were taken over by all-American Topps – best known for baseball and American football cards – the colour schemes suddenly took on a brighter aspect, designs were borrowed from US issues, and cool little footballs let you know whether Jack Ashurst played defense, off-fense or quarterback.

They were derailed by the distinctly European Panini come 1978, mind, and that three-cards-in-one budget issue was a sorry low. Gary Rowell reduced to one-third of a card...

Petrol Station Paradise

As much as we love Esso for their regular forecourt forays into football freebies, back in 1972 many of us grew a little less innocent at the hands of the friendly fossil-fuel floggers. That is when we and everyone we knew at school were mysteriously unable to complete our set of these

fantastic foil football badges. We'd all successfully collected 50, but 26 were still missing. And, curiously, it was the same 26 vacant spaces on everyone's big blue board.

Up until then, we'd politely declined Esso's invitation to buy a 'starter pack' of 26 badges for 20p; but the next time Dad dropped by for his weekly two quid's worth of 4-star, we pleaded and promised to cut the lawn... and the hedge... and so learned an early lesson about something for nothing, marketing and

the caring, sharing oil industry. But, far more importantly, we'd got the full set!

Wembley Woes

Sunderland made five Wembley appearances in the '80s and '90s and lost each one. We can quickly dismiss the Football League Centenary Tournament defeat on penalties by Wigan Athletic in 1988. The qualifying conditions would take forever to explain, games were of a 40-minute duration followed by penalties, if needed. They were needed in Sunderland's case as they went out in front of a crowd of just 41,500 in the 100,000 capacity stadium. Bearing in mind that 16 teams (including Newcastle) took part in day one of the two-day competition, tickets were hardly scarce and it was a poor weekend for the ticket touts, not just for our Colin Pascoe who missed the decisive penalty.

Three years previously Sunderland made their first appearance in a League Cup final, then known as the Milk Cup. Just over a week earlier the Lads walloped the Canaries 3-1 at Carrow Road. All the fans said, "It would be just like us to go and lose at Wembley." They were right. A Clive Walker missed penalty and a Gordon Chisholm own-goal meant a miserable journey back up north while Steve Bruce and his team-mates

paraded the trophy and prepared for European football the following season.

Then everything unravelled. Both teams ended the season disastrously and were relegated to Division Two. In May the Bradford City stadium fire saw 56 lives lost, followed only 18 days later by Heysel where 39 mainly Juventus fans were killed. As a consequence, English clubs, including Norwich, were banned from competing in Europe.

1990 was the first year that Play-off finals were held at Wembley, and Sunderland were up against Swindon Town. Both clubs had finished the season on 74 points but Swindon finished fourth on goal difference, two places ahead of the Lads. We were definitely on a high, having beaten Newcastle in the semi-final.

The weather was good but so were Swindon – very, very good. The only goal of the game was scored in the 27th minute by Town's Alan McLoughlin but the scoreline could have been much worse were it not for the heroics of keeper Tony Norman. The goal took a heavy deflection from Gary Bennett, who was making history that day as the first black player to captain a League side at Wembley.

The journey home was once again miserable.

Fans were vaguely aware that Swindon were due to face

charges of making illegal payments just ten days later but no one had any expectation that this would influence in which Division we'd be spending the 1990/91 season.

Swindon pleaded guilty to 35 of the 36 charges made against them and were duly relegated to Division Three (this was later reduced to relegation to Division Two). Sunderland had strong claims to take Swindon's place in the top Division; but the Magpies claimed it should be them as they'd finished fourth in Division Two, and Sheffield Wednesday tried desperately to cling on to their First Division spot, arguing for a reprieve because they had occupied the final relegation place. It was July, and much biting of nails ensued before everything was resolved and Sunderland, for once, appeared to have luck on their side. We were promoted! Although that was as far as our lucky breaks went, as we were relegated the following season.

We were soon back at Wembley, this time for the 1992 FA Cup final against Liverpool.

I didn't have a season ticket that year and only got to the match by the skin of my teeth. With less than 24 hours to kick-off I learned there was a ticket available in Leeds. I was working in London so jumped on a train to pick up the ticket and got the next train straight back down south.

I'd forgotten to ask which part of the ground the ticket was for and found myself in what was nominally the Liverpool end but, as ever, hundreds of Mackems had somehow found their way into the opposition's territory.

The game felt like an anti-climax. It was definitely winnable. It wasn't a particularly good Liverpool side; they'd finished sixth in Division One and we had our chances to go ahead in the first half, particularly one that fell to John Byrne. But it was also far from a vintage Sunderland squad, and two second-half goals saw the Scousers coast home.

The most heartbroken I've ever felt after a match was our next Wembley appearance, the 1998 play-off final against Charlton. We had a great season and travelled in hope (expectation is too strong a word when it comes to Sunderland) that we would soon be competing with Man United, Liverpool, Arsenal – the big boys.

I'm not in the habit of writing to football managers but a few years earlier I'd written to Denis Smith urging him to sign a Mackem called Clive Mendonca who was then struggling to get into the Sheffield United side. The very same Mendonca scored a hat trick in a ridiculously see-saw epic which ended 4-4. After 13 successful spot-kicks, Mickey Gray's sudden-death penalty was saved by Charlton keeper Sasa Ilic, and we kept up our record of not having won at Wembley since 1973.

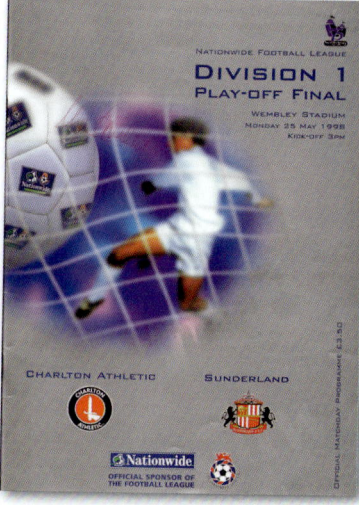

The faces in cars going up the M1 and A1 that evening said it all. Instead of the big boys next season it would be more of Crewe, Tranmere and Grimsby. Every cloud has a silver lining though, and the 1998/99 season would give us some of the most exhilarating football we've experienced in a lifetime of following the Lads.

The Badge

The story of the Sunderland badge is far from straightforward. In common with most clubs a badge wasn't considered a priority in the first half of the 20th century. The only occasion deemed worthy of bothering to put a crest on the shirt was the FA Cup final, so in 1913 and 1937 Sunderland wore versions of the County Borough of Sunderland's arms, featuring the sextant and globe.

Another version of this appeared on the front of the programme from 1953 to 1966, and with the cover unchanging for 13

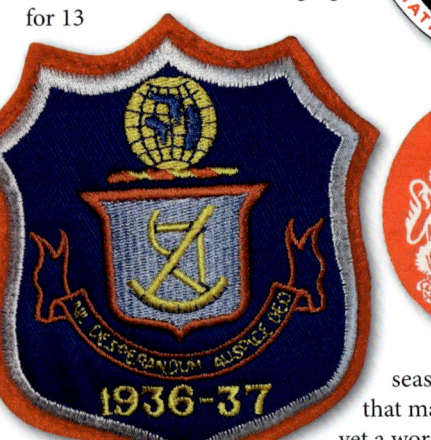

seasons you can detect that marketing wasn't yet a word that appeared in

football's vocabulary.

But England's World Cup win in 1966 would change all that as football suddenly became very marketable. In the late '60s two different badges were appearing on club literature: the black cat standing on a ball and the graphic shield design, but neither appeared on the shirts. The only badge worn was an SAFC monogram that was worn on the red away kit.

In 1972 the club finally came up with a new and definitive club badge, the ship, which appeared on the front of the programme. But it didn't make it on to the front of the shirts for another five years. Umbro had a fashion for script initials at the time, as worn by Leeds, Everton, Burnley and many others. So it was this

embroidered 'SAFC' that was worn at Wembley in the 1973 FA Cup final.

The ship badge eventually made it on to the players' chests in 1977 and remained there for two decades, albeit in several different versions. The brown and yellow were removed, followed by the blue, until the badge truly reflected the club colours of red, white and black.

The departure from Roker Park heralded a new badge for a new age and they threw a lot in there, but came up with a pleasing design, although not one easily carved into your school desk.

The black cat had been upgraded to two lions, the Wearmouth Bridge

and Penshaw Monument both featured, along with a pit wheel, a nod to the Stadium of Light's location where once had stood the Monkwearmouth Colliery.

It may be a sobering thought to supporters of a certain age that this 'new' club crest has now had a longer lifespan than the ship badge!

Wearbeat

In the early 1960s Sunderland emerged from the tunnel at Roker Park to a stirring rendition of the *Z-Cars* theme tune. The music is more often associated with Everton, who still use it, and the song on which the tune is based – 'Johnny Todd' – has its roots in Liverpool, so perhaps they do have the greatest claim for ownership. Watford adopted the tune in 1964, a year or two after the Toffees and the Lads. It's still played every other week when the Hornets appear at Vicarage Road.

Sunderland moved on from the TV theme tune, and we're now most closely associated with two pieces of music – Prokofiev's 'Dance of the Knights' and Elvis Presley's 'Can't Help Falling in Love' – so wise men say...

A lot of away fans thought Sunderland were being pretentious, playing classical music while the teams lined up in the tunnel at the Stadium of Light, but more than 25 years after its introduction it still sends a shiver down my spine. In any case, Mackems have always had that extra touch of class.

The music switches to Republica's 'Ready to Go' as the

players cross the touchline and, seconds before the kick-off, the strains of Elvis ring around the ground. A great start to the clash that lies ahead.

There have of course been the usual FA Cup final releases. 1973 saw the Lads combine with Sunderland-born comedian Bobby Knoxall to record 'Sunderland All The Way', with the immortal lines "Sunderland will be in the First Division / scoring goals in every game they play / Sunderland will be in the First Division / it'll be red and white all the way."

Deciding that a cover of a previous hit stood more chance of chart success, the 1992 Cup final squad recorded McFadden & Whitehead's 'Ain't No Stopping Us Now'. Music lovers the world over wished that someone had indeed stopped them – from the stomping destruction of a '70s classic.

That Mackem touch of class emerged again in 1998 when 'Choral Passions', the original soundtrack from

the TV documentary *Premier Passions,* was released as a single; but sadly the rest of the country weren't refined enough for it to rocket up the charts.

Indeed, the famed 'hotbed of football' became a hotbed of music, so much so that in 1997 Cherry Red Records brought out a 20-track CD featuring classics like 'Gannin't Roker Park' by Ronnie Roker and the Black Cats, 'The Dickie Ord Song' by the puntastically named Simply Red and White, and 'I Left My Heart in Roker Park' by Alfie.

The release was spurred by Simply Red and White's

unlikely 1996 chart hit, 'Cheer Up Peter Reid'. And so we move in traditional pub style straight from the raucous singalongs to the hotly contested music quiz:

1) What number did the aforementioned 'Cheer Up Peter Reid' reach in the national charts? It's more than respectable, all things considered!

2) Which American group sang the original 'Daydream Believer', which the Sunderland song is based on?

3) Which classic rock band dropped into the new stadium opening ceremony in a helicopter back in 1997?

Answers:
1) 41!
2) The Monkees.
3) Status Quo.

The Scrapper

A big crinkly book full of yellowing newsprint, yellower glue and spent, sticky-free Sellotape. That's all that we're left with today – a tatty relic of golden childhood days.

But the past, so we're reliably informed, is another country, and the seemingly humble scrapbook was once about as much fun as any junior football fan could possibly imagine.

Long before the invention of the 24-hour kids' TV channel, the internet and video games, young people had a

relatively vast amount of time on our hands. And we filled it with memories in the form of stuck-in autographs, tickets, and football cards that would now be worth a small fortune if only we'd simply kept them in mint condition.

Most of us have had a go at assembling scraps devoted to our favourite football team, but few persisted for very long.

The first page of every

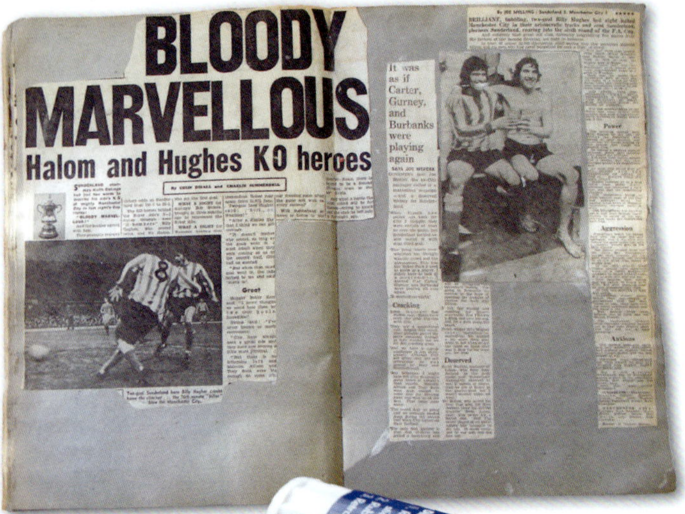

scrapbook is filled,
the last page hardly
ever.

After a few weeks, cutting match
reports and photos out of the paper tended
to become a chore, enabling you to later track the ever-
decreasing degree of care with which they were Gloyed on
to the coarse pages.

The misguided attempt to stick in 3-D objects such as
badges, rosettes and (you can take this as a confession)
seashells led to a particularly unsatisfying, lumpy scrapper.

And then there was that final time you jumped the gun
and Dad found a comedy hole in the back of his *Sunday
Mirror* before he'd finished with it...

Just Ask

When we were kids there was a saying among adults, "Those who ask, don't get." I always thought this was arrant nonsense and dangerously subservient. Young Sunderland fan Mark obviously felt the same way. He fancied a look at the FA Cup, so he asked. And Bob Stokoe was only too happy to help. "Come down one morning next week and ask for Mr Bailey." Marvellous!

SUNDERLAND ASSOCIATION FOOTBALL CLUB
LIMITED (REGISTERED No. 49116 ENGLAND)

REGISTERED OFFICES AND GROUND,
ROKER PARK GROUND, SUNDERLAND, SR6 9SW.

MANAGER: R. STOKOE, SECRETARY: R. M. LINNEY, COMMERCIAL MANAGER: G. H. DIMBLEBY,
TELEPHONE NOS. 72077 & 58638, TELEGRAPHIC ADDRESS: 'FOOTBALL, SUNDERLAND.'

RS/BKB

8th August, 1973.

Houghton le Spring.

Dear Mark,

You can certainly come to Roker Park and have a look at the F.A. Cup. If you come down one morning next week and ask for Mr. Bailey he will show the Cup to you.

Best wishes.

Yours sincerely,

B.K. Brain

R. STOKOE
p.p. MANAGER

Asics

Not a lot of people know that ASICS is an acronym for the Latin 'Anima Sana in Corpore Sano' – although I'm sure you could be persuaded to join me in 'praying for a healthy mind in a healthy body'...

We have Peris Hatton, author of *The Shirt Hunter* ('one man's ceaseless pursuit of classic football shirts') to thank for the inside information on the inner meaning of our old shirts, as well as their background. The company was founded in Japan where it was originally known as Onitsuka, only switching to its current name in 1977, when

Asics was better known in the world of athletics.

Although they'd been around the English and Scottish leagues since the end of the 1980s, producing shirts for the likes of Norwich City, Coventry City and both Dundee clubs, it's far more important to us that Asics went on to storm the British football shirt market in the early '90s, a golden age when the brand and logo became very handily synonymous with Blackburn Rovers' rise to become the Premier League winners in 1994/95.

Our two Asics home shirts are hugely evocative to any Sunderland fan who was around to see them in action, as their three-year reign coincided with

the opening of the Stadium of Light in 1997/98 and the high drama of that season's Wembley finale, the ensuing points fest in 1998/99 and a seventh-place Premier League finish in 1999/00. Three out of three great seasons: not too shoddy.

And the same goes for the beautiful quality of the shirts, made of the finest, thickest, softest nylon I think I've ever felt. And great design, too: have we ever had a better second strip than the Asics navy with red and white hoops?

The Roker Roar

Kingdom by the Sea is an enthusiastic and knowledgeable 1960s Northeast guidebook by the wonderful Betty James, who also wrote the inspirational *London On £1 A Day*. Betty is tempted to Roker Park by the draw of Chelsea, her own 'home town' team, and by the question of 'whether football is a game the little woman is ever likely to understand'.

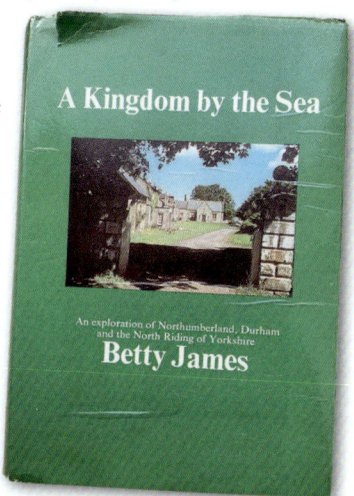

Betty samples a hot-dog as reinforced boots trample her frozen tootsies. But the excitement soon hots up.

"The music gets louder, vintage rattles and car hooters are produced. A lethal-looking banner is unfurled under my left ear. Two fifty-seven p.m. and excitement has reached fever pitch. The music blares louder, people start pushing. There's a roar, an orgiastic swaying of bodies and they're off!"

Betty is poked in the eye, her tonsure is ruffled and she drops her second hot-dog when her head is caught in a two-man pelvic grip, the Roker Roar ringing in her ears:

"'Dir-TEE Dir-TEE… Ooooo grotty. It's pa-THE-tic.'
"'Nice ball nice nice nice. OOOOO!'
"'What a bloody way to play!'"

The Leagueliner

The Leagueliner was a 12-carriage train designed specifically to transport football fans to away games. Each club could book the train for the day and the club was then left to organise everything from timings to catering.

In January 1973 Burnley were the first set of fans to experience the delights of the on-board discotheque, cinema and music coaches complete with headphones.

The Sunderland programme for the home game against Cardiff on 8th September 1973 had boasted in bold upper case "FIRST OF THE BIG 3 TO USE THE LEAGUELINER." In case you are wondering, the other big two were the Magpies and Middlesbrough. It does seem an empty boast though – we used the train before you did? It's on a par with Newcastle fans claiming they support a bigger club than Sunderland because they have an airport.

The big event was the trip to West Bromwich on 29th September. The return fare to Birmingham was £3.50 but for another 50p a packed lunch could be yours while you travelled 'in comfort with Disco, Meals, Bar and

	LEAGUELINER.			
DEPART.	NEWCASTLE	SUNDERLAND	SEAHAM	HARTLEPOOL
	7-30a.m.	7-55a.m.	8-07a.m.	8-29a.m.
ARRIVE BIRMINGHAM	12-20p.m.			
DEPART BIRMINGHAM	6-00p.m.			
ARRIVE	10-56p.m.	10-29p.m.	10-18p.m.	9-55p.m.

Restaurant'. I don't know what happened to the cinema.

The train left Sunderland Station before breakfast and got back around 10.30pm. The game, a 1-1 draw, was more eventful than the train journey and by September 1976 the Leagueliner was consigned to the scrapheap.

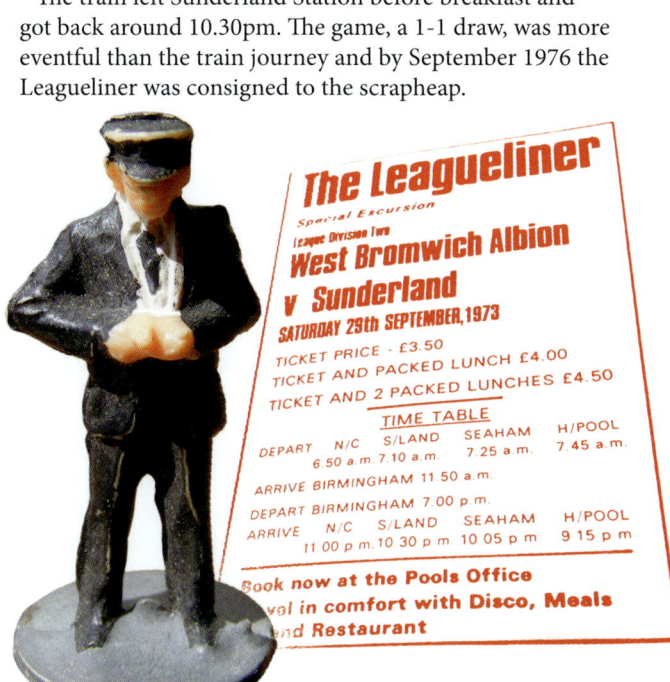

Testimonials

A player normally became entitled to a testimonial after serving the same club for at least ten years, or if their career was ended prematurely by injury. They were commonplace at one time. Seven of the 1963/64 promotion-winning team were with the Lads for ten years or more. That wouldn't happen nowadays. Too many agents and too much money. In any event, how could a millionaire footballer expect the ordinary man/woman/child in the street to contribute to a little-needed nest egg at the end of their career?

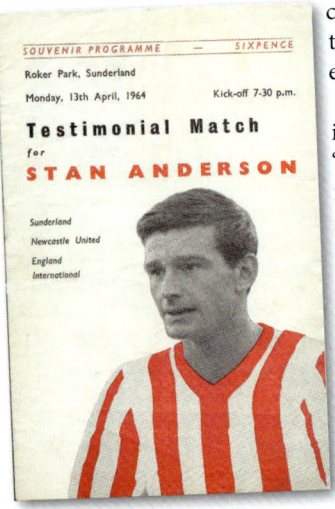

Stan Anderson's testimonial in April 1964 was the first 'big game' I ever attended. It followed the tradition of being relatively non-competitive. Sunderland took on an International XI including several players who had been capped by England. That the 'all-stars' included Jackie Milburn and Bobby Mitchell who were both aged 39 and long since retired, shows the spirit in which the game was played. A crowd of almost 28,000 turned up to pay their respects to Stan who spent much of his career under the constraints of the maximum wage. Testimonials were meant for loyal players like Stan Anderson.

It's hard to believe but there was a period when derbies were considered suitable as testimonial games. They were certainly money-spinners for the players concerned but guaranteed crowd trouble.

Newcastle's Ollie Burton was lucky enough to have arranged a testimonial match against a Sunderland side fresh from their Wembley triumph in May 1973. The Cup-winners attracted a crowd of 35,873 to St James Park. Newcastle were 2-0 up with 20 minutes to go when we noticed a lot of Magpies coming into our part of the ground. My message to my three mates was, "Hide your scarves. This is a meaningless friendly. If we score, do not, I repeat do not, jump up." This was the cue for Ron Guthrie to hit the back of the net, and for the idiot next to me to celebrate as if we'd hit a last-minute winner in a Play-off final. To say we left the ground in a hurry would be putting it mildly.

International XI

Shirts—White, trimmed with Black, Red and Black bands.
Shorts—Scarlet. Stockings—Red, White and Black

Eddie Hopkinson
Bolton Wanderers and England

Ken Shellito   Gordon Jones
Chelsea and England   *Middlesbrough and England Under 23*

Stan Anderson   John Sleeuwenhoek   Bobby Robson
Newcastle United   *Aston Villa*   *Fulham*
and England   *and England Under 23*   *and England*

Dave Hilley   George Eastham
Newcastle United   *Arsenal*
and Scotland Under 23   *and England*

Bryan Douglas   Jackie Milburn   Bobby Mitchell
Blackburn Rovers   *Newcastle United*   *Newcastle United*
and England   *and England*   *and Scotland*

Referee—   Linesmen—
Mr. R. T. E. LANGDALE,   Mr. J. O'NEIL, South Shields
Darlington.   Mr. J. BUTLER, Sunderland.

George Mulhall   Dominic Sharkey   Brian Usher

Johnny Crossan   George Herd

Jimmy McNab   Charlie Hurley   Martin Harvey

Len Ashurst   Cecil Irwin

Jimmy Montgomery

Shorts—White.   Shirts—Red and White Stripes.
                Stockings—Red with White tops.
Sunderland

The following year Monty was the beneficiary of the Sunderland vs Newcastle testimonial. Just under 30,000 people were at Roker Park to pay tribute to one of the best keepers of all time.

Sadly, for many of the players that followed, the police put paid to these 'friendly' derby clashes. In 1996 Dicky Ord had a testimonial against Middlesbrough planned when the police said "no." He had to settle for a fixture against Steaua Bucharest. Adverts for the game tried to arouse interest by adding '(six internationals)' after Steaua's name but the Wearside public was not impressed, and only 8,808 turned up to watch an uninspiring and bad tempered match.

In March 1977 Billy Hughes reverted to having International All Stars as the opposition for his

testimonial. It was end-to-end stuff as the All Stars, featuring 39-year-old Bobby Charlton, ended 6-3 winners. Timing is everything though, and Billy's special day came as Sunderland were joint bottom of Division One and headed for relegation. The crowd of just over 6,400 reflected the public's disillusionment with their club. Only 12 months earlier, with Sunderland buoyant after gaining promotion, Bobby Kerr's testimonial attracted four times as many as Billy's.

A Monday night late in November does not seem the ideal time of year for a testimonial but that was the fate that befell Ritchie Pitt and Bobby Park who shared a testimonial against Dutch side AZ '67 in 1975. Both players had suffered career-ending injuries, and the takings from the match were meant to partly compensate for their loss of earnings. Both had been tipped for international honours before their injuries. There were no 'all stars' or cavalier football as the two sides played out a goalless bore draw for the 7,874 faithful that had bothered to turn up.

The biggest testimonial to be held at the Stadium of Light falls outside of the period covered by this book but mention should be made of Niall Quinn's benefit match on 14th May 2002. 'Disco Pants' created a precedent in

donating all of the takings (over £1 million) to children's charities.

Niall's gesture was even subject to an Early Day Motion in the House of Commons on 21st January 2002.

"That this House applauds the decision of the footballer Niall Quinn, Sunderland striker and Republic of Ireland international, to donate all proceeds from his testimonial match to children's hospitals in Sunderland and Dublin; supports his intention to encourage fellow players in the testimonial match, to be played between Sunderland and the Republic of Ireland at the Stadium of Light, to sponsor individual children in developing countries and to take a personal interest in their future; notes that Niall Quinn's charitable actions are likely to raise over one million pounds which will benefit children on both sides of the Irish Sea; and hopes that other footballers and individuals in jobs attracting significant bonuses will be inspired to follow his hugely generous example."

The Motion was signed by 52 MPs including one Conservative member. Hats off to Dr Julian Lewis, Tory MP for New Forest East.

Crake, Rattle & Roll

The football rattle – or 'crake' as it's sometimes known locally – enjoyed its heyday in the 1960s, when they became as iconic a symbol of football-supporterdom as the scarf and bobble-hat, all three long since consigned to the dustbin of fashion and football history.

They first came in after WWI, a relic of the trenches; but later models were most often homemade, employing the sort of engineering skills that only Dad could manage,

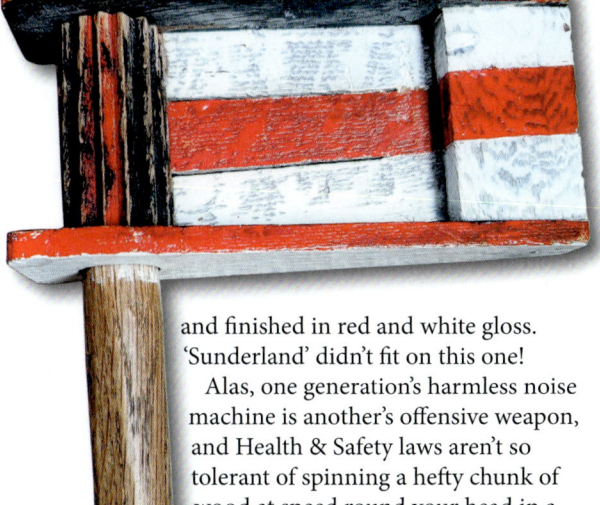

and finished in red and white gloss. 'Sunderland' didn't fit on this one!

Alas, one generation's harmless noise machine is another's offensive weapon, and Health & Safety laws aren't so tolerant of spinning a hefty chunk of wood at speed round your head in a tightly packed crowd. You could have someone's eye out.

Season Tickets

Season tickets, or 'season cards' as they're known by the younger generation, used to be the exception rather than the rule. Payment, by cash, at the turnstile, was very much the norm. With currently around 38,000 season-ticket holders at the Stadium of Light, there's much less scope for the casual supporter to stroll across on matchday whenever the mood should take them.

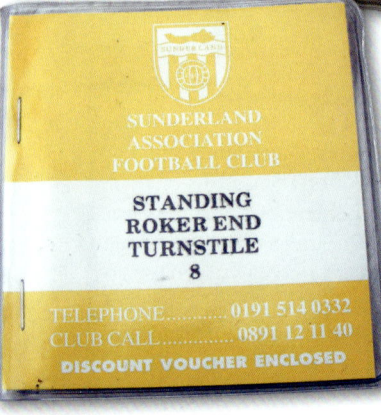

Season tickets come from a much calmer and simpler time. Each year the season-ticket holder was sent a plastic wallet containing a number of detachable tickets, each with a number that denoted the match for which entry was sought.* There were tickets for reserve

games, too, and spares in the case of a cup run. These were rarely used, or necessary.

We knew the match number because a sign above each turnstile would proclaim: 'Match Number XX'.

Sunderland adopted a straightforward approach. The first match was match number 1, then we had match number 2, 3, and so on until we got to match number 21 and the end of another season. Leeds United, in what I've always considered an unnecessarily spiteful act, used random numbers so the first match of the season could have required any ticket number between 1 and 21. Their reasoning was that this would prevent season-ticket holders sharing tickets with friends. But ha! The flaw in this high-tech security system was exposed when fans simply lent their entire book to whoever they wished.

On or around the 2009/10 season, traditional tear-out paper season tickets were replaced by a plastic card. The term 'season card' is no doubt factually accurate but I still think it sounds a little pompous. The card itself carries the title of 'Season Access Card.' For goodness' sake, it's a season ticket!

The move to a card was not a popular one, and was greeted with much suspicion, but that was nothing compared to the furore in the early 2020s when we were asked to gain admittance using a mobile phone.

Since this latest technological 'enhancement', the most stressful part of my matchday experience is the 15 minutes leading up to gaining entry to the stadium. I check

my phone, look for the electronic wallet, find a QR code (is that even the correct term?) and pray that I put the phone in the right place and the turnstile clicks open.

My fears came home to roost on 23rd September 2023. No click. I was banished to queue at the ticket office, along with a few hundred others. The bad news was, I didn't get to my seat until 53 minutes into the game; but this was alleviated by the fact I hadn't missed any goals. However, I was there in the 87th minute when Cardiff scored the only goal of the game.

Bring back season tickets.

*Except, apparently, for directors who had a single card covering all the matches – see above.

Calendar Boys

most clubs recognise that calendars make handy presents, and Sunderland are no exception. But how much thought is given about which players to include, and when? The calendar year runs from January to December but the football 'year' is August to May.

As you open your new calendar on Christmas Day the January transfer window is not far off. If your player for the month of January is coveted by other clubs, his inclusion on the calendar is surely an indication of confidence that he'll still be with us after the window eases shut.

A useful rule of thumb is for clubs to include their rubbish players in the latter months of the year, just in case all the good ones leave in August. The manager may be left with a queue of disgruntled players wanting to know why they are Mr September, October, November or December.

The last thing a club wants is to have a player leave before his month as the face of the calendar arrives.

Alarmingly, 2006 saw Sunderland manage to include five players who had played their last game for the club by the time their turn came to adorn thousands of bedroom walls.

One of the five was Alan Stubbs, who had joined from Everton the previous August. His time on Wearside was undistinguished, culminating in allegations that while out injured he celebrated a late Everton winner against Sunderland at the Stadium of Light. Stubbs denied all claims but did still attract feelings of disdain. Problem was, he was Mr March – by which time he had rejoined Everton.

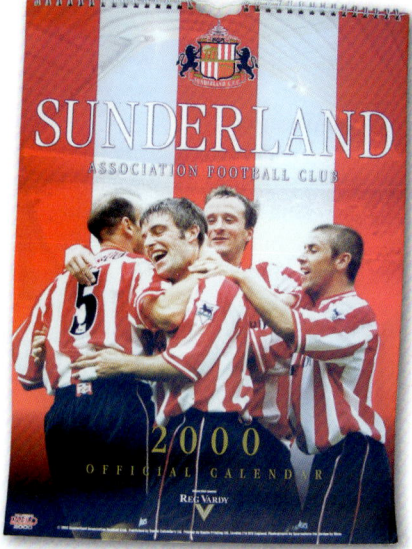

Some fans simply gave Mr February (Justin Hoyte) two months on their wall. Others fast-forwarded to April (Gary Breen). Many scribbled a comical moustache on the tainted Scouser or placed a blanket over the offending 31 days.

The other four who lasted longer on the calendar than in the first team were Christian Bassila, Andy Gray, Kelvin Davis and Jon Stead. Like Stubbs, all were signed in August 2005. Can there ever have been a worse calendar selection or, indeed, a less successful batch of signings?

My Favourite XI - 1965-1999

Goalkeeper
Jimmy Montgomery. By far the easiest choice to make. If I was naming an All-Time World XI Monty would still be in the team. He gained national acclaim for his double save at Wembley but Sunderland fans know he regularly made saves like that while keeping Sunderland in the First Division almost single handed, season after season.

Defence
Barry Venison. We haven't been blessed with outstanding full backs but Venison just squeezes out Chris Makin for the right back position. Captained the team as a 20-year-old in the 1985 Milk Cup final and went on to play for England, albeit after he had left Sunderland having made exactly 200 appearances for the club.

Michael Gray. With long flowing locks like Venison, the pair could be mistaken for twins. They could switch wings and bamboozle the opposition but there might be a tussle for the hair dryer in the changing room at full-time. An England international, only six players have played more times for

Sunderland than Michael Gray. Joe Bolton just missed out on selection.

Charlie Hurley. Impossible to omit our 'Player of the 20th Century' known to one and all as The King. A towering presence in the side and definitely the captain, he was a born leader. Played 400 times for the Lads and 40 times for the Republic of Ireland. He once walked down our street in Millfield, no idea why, or where he was going, but he was a colossus.

Dave Watson. I'm not sure how well Hurley and Watson would have gelled. They were similar players but how can I leave out a player who won 65 caps for England and was arguably Man of the Match in the 1973 FA Cup final. We certainly wouldn't lose any headers at the back and would terrify opposing defences from corners and set pieces.

Colin Todd. Class and composure personified. A place had to be found for 'Toddoso', I see him playing in front of Hurley and Watson and, as Brian Clough once said, "Colin Todd can play anywhere." Made almost 200 appearances for the Lads but was at his peak during nine seasons at Derby.

Midfield

Jim Baxter. Many say 'Slim Jim' was past his best when he came to Roker. Perhaps he was, but he was a Sunderland player in 1967 when he played keepie-up at Wembley as Scotland beat England 3-2. He didn't look like a has-been that day or any other days I can remember. He oozed class and made the game look easy. One of the best penalty takers I have ever seen – up there with Gary Rowell and Martin Scott.

Tony Towers. Towers first made an impact on Sunderland when he scored Manchester City's opening goal in the 2-2 draw at Maine Road in the 1973 FA Cup run. He was later sent off after a clash with Micky Horswill. When Towers joined Sunderland in March 1974 Horswill moved to City as part of the deal which may have been a good thing if either of them bore a grudge. Hard working with a powerful shot, Towers played for England while still with Sunderland.

Dennis Tueart. My favourite player ever. He could do everything; run, tackle, head, shoot, you name it and Tueart had it in his repertoire. Easily as good as his contemporary Kevin Keegan, Tueart chose to join New York Cosmos while at his peak.

Keegan stayed closer to home and the British media by joining Hamburg. As a result, Keegan won 63 England caps while Tueart, starring in the less fashionable and arguably less competitive North American Soccer League, picked up a mere six.

Forwards

Kevin Phillips. Although a member of England's unsuccessful Euro 2000 squad, he didn't make it on to the pitch. Had he done so I'm sure he would have shone on the big stage and ended up somewhere like Real Madrid. In 1999/2000 Super Kev scored an amazing 30 Premier League goals and became the first English player to win the European Golden Shoe. After Monty, he would be the first name on my teamsheet.

Niall Quinn. Would he have got into my fantasy team if he wasn't playing alongside Kevin Phillips? The answer is "probably." Marco Gabbiadini was another of my favourite ever players and a real contender for the best XI but there was a lot more to Quinny than height, heading ability and lay-offs. He had a brilliant touch and scored some real beauties. A former player, manager and chairman, he ticks all the boxes and will always be a true Sunderland legend.

Bob

Outside the Stadium of Light stands what is, in my unbiased opinion, the best statue at any football ground. Bob Stokoe is captured forever sprinting across the Wembley turf following the glorious FA Cup win against Leeds.

Bob had only been in charge at Roker for six months when he landed the club's first major honour in 36 years. And then he followed that up with promotion to the first division in 1975/76, cementing his place in the Sunderland Pantheon of demi-gods.

At this point, we can't ignore the photo of Stokoe in the Newcastle shirt, the club for which he clocked up 261 appearances, including the victorious 1955 FA Cup final.

I should also remind readers that there were two ex-Mags in the '73 final squad: Ron Guthrie and David Young. And there were two players, Stan Anderson and Alan Foggon, who managed to play for all three North East clubs around this time.

Sometimes you have to turn a blind eye, although it doesn't always go well. Remember Lee Clark having to leave Sunderland in 1999 after being photographed in a 'Sad Mackem Bas***ds" T-shirt?

But safe to say Bob was loved by both sets of fans, as you could see by the attendance at his funeral in 2004.

Kids in Kits

It was a magic feeling, pulling on your team's shirt, shorts and socks. And then looking down at the badge. It was the kind of occasion that warranted pestering your mother to get the camera out.

"Mam, take it now. Take it while I'm doing this..."

Waiting impatiently between shots while she 'wound it on'. Standing up with your arms folded, or with one foot on the ball... then

it wasn't your mam any more, it was the official club photographer on photocall day, taking the photo that would appear in *Shoot!* or on a football sticker. Or else you were your club's brand new signing, and a gaggle of snappers from the dailies were crowded round.

"I think I've come to the end of the film," says Mam as

her winder-onner meets resistance.

"Take it anyway!"...

Young Andy Dawson provides us with a great example of the art, snapped on his

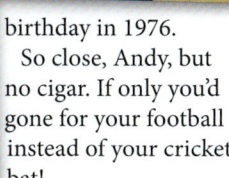

birthday in 1976.

So close, Andy, but no cigar. If only you'd gone for your football instead of your cricket bat!

The other kids in kits are my sons, Adam (above) and Gareth at various ages. Crikey, I must have spent a fortune in that club shop, over the years...

Charlie Buchan

It isn't every club that can say one of their most illustrious old boys was the man behind the world's first monthly football magazine, unleashed on Britain's thrill-starved youth in September 1951. Charlie Buchan scored over 200 goals in a Sunderland career that spanned WWI, and notched four in six for England, for good measure.

His ground-breaking *Football Monthly* injected some colour into the grey post-war landscape, albeit by daubing vivid pastel hues over black-and-white photos. In an era when kids were only expected to speak when spoken to, Charlie undid the top button of his sports jacket and did his best to address the herberts.

Even from the standpoint of 75 years on, the magazine's format is strikingly familiar, suggesting Charlie's editorial team got it pretty much right first time. There's analysis and tips from ex-pros and other enthusiastic scribblers; there's page-size posters for the bedroom wall, and interviews with players who aren't allowed to say anything.

Thumbing now through Buchan's back pages, he provides a unique window into an unrecognisable world of side partings and V-neck shirts, of rugby boots and weirdly recoloured violet irises. And there was more than just the magazine to the CB empire, with hardback annuals proving popular Christmas stocking fillers for decades. Likewise the reissued 'best of' annuals which have lit up the football nostalgia market over recent years.

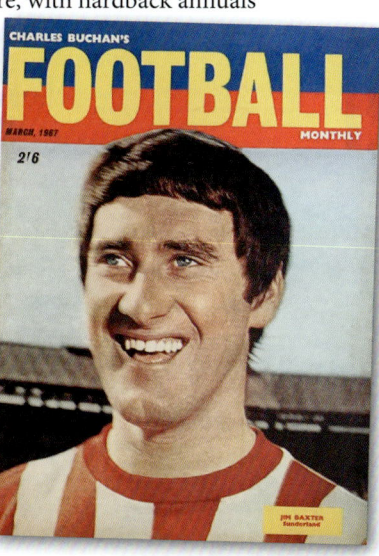

From the magazine's perspective, football was steering into choppy waters when Buchan died in 1960, leaving the *Monthly* rudderless in the face of tidal changes such as footballers seeking the end of the minimum wage, and suddenly not all agreeing to sport Brylcreemed hair.

Finally, the originator's name was dropped from the title as more modern arrivals thrived; but it was great while it lasted.

Zine Scene

Following on from the music-led revolution in DIY publishing, it took a while for football to catch up, but eventually fans took to their cranky old typewriters, hunting and pecking and ker-chinging out their frustrations, and learning all-new reprographic skills along the way. They were

NOT A REGULAR SIGHT

tired of hearing 'The Fans' View' expressed second hand in the media by journalists whose papers and radio shows were reliant on the clubs themselves, the FA and the Football League.

Untamed and fiercely independent, the first wave of fanzine rebels offered an all-new diet of uncensored opinion cut with terrace humour, aiming to reflect the views of the average fan. I was working in

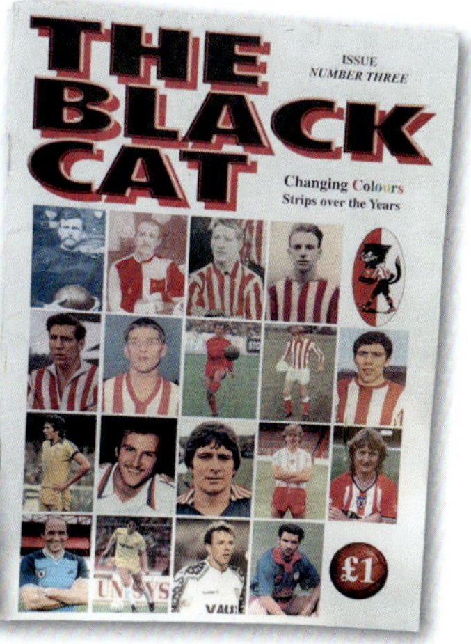

London at the time and every week I would pop down to the wonderful, now much-missed Sports Pages bookshop in Charing Cross Road and pick up a handful of fanzines with fascinating titles such as *The Memoirs of Seth Bottomley* (Port Vale, in case you wondered), *Grorty Dick* (West Bromwich) and, my personal favourite, *Abandon Chip* (McCain sponsored Scarborough).

No club was better served by fanzines than Sunderland. Peter Slater, recognised as the leading authority on fanzines and the host of the website footballfanzineculture.blog, identified 22 fanzines which focussed on the club. No Mackem could complain about being short of reading material on their favourite team.

Peter believes *Wise Men Say* was our first fanzine. It launched in 1987, cost 40p and ran for 17 issues until 1991. Its initial publication coincided with our first ever season in Division Three. The state of some of the grounds came

as a bit of a culture shock, leading to articles such as a review of travels around the grounds entitled 'To Hell and Back (Via Scunthorpe)'. I don't miss those days.

The multi-award-winning *A Love Supreme* followed soon afterwards, and is still thriving as one of the very few remaining printed fanzines in the country.

We also had our share of quirkily named fanzines. *Sex and Chocolate Aren't As Good As Football* (an offshoot of *A Love Supreme*) inevitably springs to mind, as does the more downbeat *It's The Hope I Can't Stand*, and *It's An Easy One For Norman* – the latter being a reference to a clanger Tony Norman dropped in an FA Cup game at Sheffield Wednesday.

The Generation Game

I wasn't particularly close to my paternal grandfather but perhaps I got my love of football from him. He was a butcher with a shop in High Street East in the east end of Sunderland. This was the sort of social standing that often earned a place in the boardroom. Arab sheiks and Russian oligarchs hadn't discovered football at that stage. Grandad wasn't a director but he had good friends who were, Jack Parker (fishmonger) and Bill Ditchburn (solicitor). Legend has it he was once banned from the directors' box because he got over-excited and pummelled someone's bowler hat.

He certainly had the 'life of Riley.' He never missed an England vs Scotland game and always attended the FA Cup final. Of course, we sang 'Abide With Me' at his funeral.

He was at Wembley in 1937 when we won the Cup for the first time. It is said he got so drunk he had to be wheeled back to King's Cross in a wheelbarrow. In 1973, now too old to travel, he watched the match on TV. The tension was all too much for him and an emergency doctor had to be called because he had sky-high blood pressure.

Now I have two grandsons, and they're following in their great grandad's footsteps. The photo shows Toby, my eldest grandson with his dad. It was taken in 2019 at Toby's first ever away game at Scunthorpe. Five generations spanning over a century – Sunderland 'til we die, and beyond.

Christmas Morning

In our day, Christmases weren't quite the same as the sumptuous Victorian festivals portrayed in TV ads, on glittery cards and chocolate boxes

We didn't have stockings hanging from huge holly-bedecked fireplaces. We had striped pillowcases stuck on the end of our beds. Our guests weren't jolly gentlemen in top hats and ladies wearing furry muffs – we had bald, moustachioed

visitors in new V-neck jumpers.

And we had flashing artificial Christmas trees, not those towering spruces portrayed on the cover of the *Radio Times*.

But even with Noel Edmonds as a televisual backdrop, Christmas morning still reached a goosebump-inducing level of excitement.

Because we knew beneath that Woolies wrapping paper lurked *Shoot!* annuals, Wembley Trophy footballs, the club video and green Subbuteo boxes.

Not many of us reached *A Christmas Carol* levels of joy, but spare a Yuletide thought for young Glyn Jefferson, pictured here in 1981 in his new Le Coq Sportif kit. "I wanted the home kit but my parents were so disgusted by the lack of proper stripes they refused to buy it!"

AUTHOR

Bill Hern is Sunderland born and bred. He watched his first League game in 1965 and saw his heroes go one up in the very first minute. 'Supporting Sunderland is going to be great,' he thought. Ninety minutes later he trudged away from Roker Park bemoaning a 2-1 defeat at the hands of a soon to be relegated Wolves.

Since then, the 1973 FA Cup win, various promotions and the current ascendancy of the club have made the disappointments and relegations bearable. Bill is an historian and a Fellow of the Royal Historical Society. His previous publications include Football's Black Pioneers – The Stories of the First Black Players to Represent the 92 League Clubs.

ACKNOWLEDGMENTS

Thanks to my mam and dad for making sure I was born in Sunderland. Supporting the Lads hasn't always been easy but the good memories outweigh the bad. Thanks to my sons Gareth and Adam and grandsons Toby and Sebastian for following in my footsteps (it's in the blood). Finally, thank you to Gary and Derek at Conker Editions for their wizardry in helping turn old bits and pieces into a treasure trove of Sunderland football history.

Image credits: 19 - James Hills; 30 - Craig Robinson; 41 - Neville Evans, NFSC; 48, 49, 61, 118 - Peris Hatton; 71, 173 - Paul Dobson; 101, 102 - Sunderland Echo - creative commons; 109 - Digital Elysium creative commons; 117 - Umbro.com; 132 - Dave Morcom; 157 - Iain Maddison; 103, 159, 161 - Mark Rennie; 186 - Andy Dawson; 194 - Glyn Jefferson; 197 - Dave Vickers (and family).

TEAMWORK

Many thanks to all our subscribers...

Barrie Calvert Goodridge | Chris Armstrong | Ann Robson
Wayne Tomlinson | Michael Kent | Michael Hall
Mike Smith | Robert Renwick | Simon Easter | Lesley Collins
David Dutton | Neil Emslie | Adrian Barber | Peter Graham
Anthony Ward | Jonathan Bottomer | Charlie Metcalf
Neal & James Hendrie | David Lown | Marshall Ritchie
Jamie Walker | Jeff Little | Lori Clark | Alan Clifton
Mark Norman Anderson | Anthony Reynolds | Dave Bell
Russell Dunbar | Laurie Brown | Jayden Hanlon
Ryan Shaun Flatley | Ian Powell | Anthony Adamiok
Peter Bolton | David J Hern | John Bains | Micky Collins
Andrew Donnelly | Keith Lawman | Raymond Cuthbertson
Graeme Cardy | Samuel McAdam | Tom Dembry | Paul King
Brian Morrison | David Armstrong | Linda Gibson
Sandra Barker | John Lane
Michael Waterson | Rob Urwin
Deborah Beattie
Ross Duncker | Peter Sixsmith
Jonnie Dance | Lucas Dance
Pat Boyle | Phil Boyle
Pete Jobling | Tony Collingwood
Ben Phillips | Paul Fenton
Paul Digby | Simon Easter
Ronnie Paul George Robson
David Metcalfe | Joel Wilson
Kelseydee Fawcett | Graeme Ostah | Keith Andrews
John Reece | Michael Kirkbride